A CASE LOAD OF COMEDY!

Brizzolaria and Strobenfenster, two Cleveland attorneys, decided that they had attained a position in the community which demanded they change their names to something simpler. So the firm's name became Booker and Booker.

One morning the receptionist received this call: "Hello, I'd like to speak to Mr. Booker, please."

"Sir," she asked, "which Mr. Booker would you like to talk to, Mr. Brizzolaria or Mr. Strobenfenster?"

* * *

PROSECUTOR: Now, tell the court how you came to take the car.

DEFENDANT: Well, it was parked in front of the cemetery, so I thought the owner was dead.

BAWDY! HILARIOUS! AND PROBABLY ILLEGAL!

THE ULTIMATE LAWYERS JOKE BOOK

BOOKS by LARRY WILDE

The *Ultimate* Jewish Joke Book
More The Official Doctors Joke Book
The Official Executives Joke Book
The Official Sports Maniacs Joke Book
The *Absolutely Last* Official Sex Maniacs Joke Book
The Official Book of John Jokes
The Official Politicians Joke Book
The Official Rednecks Joke Book
The *Last* Official Smart Kids Joke Book
The *Absolutely Last* Official Polish Joke Book
The *Last* Official Irish Joke Book
The *Last* Official Sex Maniacs Joke Book
The Larry Wilde Book of Limericks
The Official Lawyers Joke Book
The Official Doctors Joke Book
More The Official Sex Maniacs Joke Book
The *Ultimate* Jewish Joke Book
The Official Bedroom/Bathroom Joke Book
More The Official Smart Kids/Dumb Parents Joke Book
The Official Book of Sick Jokes
More The Official Jewish/Irish Joke Book
The *Last* Official Italian Joke Book
The Official Cat Lovers/Dog Lovers Joke Book
The Official Dirty Joke Book
The *Last* Official Polish Joke Book
The Official Golfers Joke Book
The Official Smart Kids/Dumb Parents Joke Book
The Official Religious/Not So Religious Joke Book
More The Official Polish/Italian Joke Book
The Official Black Folks/White Folks Joke Book
The Official Virgins/Sex Maniacs Joke Book
The Official Jewish/Irish Joke Book
The Official Polish/Italian Joke Book and in hardcover
THE COMPLETE BOOK OF ETHNIC HUMOR
HOW THE GREAT COMEDY WRITERS CREATE
   LAUGHTER
THE GREAT COMEDIANS TALK ABOUT COMEDY

THE
Ultimate
LAWYERS
JOKE
BOOK

Larry
Wilde

BANTAM BOOKS
TORONTO · NEW YORK · LONDON · SYDNEY · AUCKLAND

Better to be a mouse in the
mouth of a cat, than a man
in the hands of a lawyer.
—Spanish Proverb

THE ULTIMATE LAWYERS JOKE BOOK
A Bantam Book / August 1987

ISBN 0-553-26736-1

Published simultaneously in the United States and Canada

---

*Bantam Books are published by Bantam Books, Inc. Its trademark, consisting
of the words ''Bantam Books'' and the portrayal of a rooster, is Registered
in U.S. Patent and Trademark Office and in other countries. Marca Registrada.
Bantam Books, Inc., 666 Fifth Avenue, New York, New York 10103.*

PRINTED IN THE UNITED STATES OF AMERICA

O   0 9 8 7 6 5 4 3 2 1

For Arthur Davis—
longtime friend, tennis
champ, and the *ultimate*
attorney.

CONTENTS

Ignorance of the law excuses
no man from practicing it.

INTRODUCTION

A Gallop Poll was conducted recently
to find out which types of employment are
the most respected. Of the twenty-four professions and career choices listed, the law
ranked twelfth. (Clergymen were the most
respected; car salesmen, the least.)

Considering the constant public outcry
about attorneys—their fees and ethics—
coming in twelfth is not too bad. They fared
better than local politicians (18th), realtors
(19th), and insurance salesmen (22nd).

Members of the bar are well aware of
their standing in the community and can
handle the poison darts of ridicule. Those
with emotional security and a sense of humor are capable of comic self-deprecation:

Supreme Court Justice Sandra Day O'Connor was addressing the graduating class at Georgetown University law school and remarked: "A commencement speech is a particularly difficult assignment. You're given no topic and are expected to inspire all the graduates with a stirring speech about nothing at all. I suppose that is why so many lawyers are asked to be commencement speakers."

There is no question that barristers can be sharp and witty. It is part of their training. Witness this confrontation between members of the legal and medical professions:

An attorney got into a discussion with a physician over the merits of their respective professions. "Now I don't mean to say that all lawyers are crooks," said the doctor, "but you've got to admit that your profession doesn't make angels of men."

"Quite true," said the lawyer, "you doctors certainly have the best of us there."

And don't think for a moment that attorneys aren't just as human as the rest of us.

With the same drives and desires and hang-ups. They even enjoy female companionship.

Colby was at a Bar Association convention and met a beautiful young woman. "Would you like to have a drink?" he asked.

She said she didn't drink.

"Would you like to go back to my room and screw?"

She said she didn't do that either.

Colby said, "How about a bale of hay?"

"Are you crazy?" said the girl. "I don't eat hay."

"Just as I thought," quipped the lawyer. "You're not fit company for man or beast."

Practitioners of law furnish an important service to society. They provide counsel and advice to those who need professional guidance.

After a consultation with an attorney, Elmer ran into his friend, Zeke. "Whatcha wanna see a lawyer for?" asked Zeke.

"I needed some advice," replied Elmer.

"Waste of money," said his

friend. "Remember when you sat in the lawyer's office, did you see all the books there? Well, what he told you, you could read in those law books and it wouldn't cost you anything."

"That's right," said Zeke, "but he knows what page it's on."

Lawyers represent different things to different people. Throughout history we've been privileged to witness the legal genius of Lincoln, Clarence Darrow, Earl Rogers and Louis Nizer. These men had high ideals, lofty integrity, and fought for the justice of the common man. But what does the common man think of lawyers in general? Here are some general comments:

A lawyer is a man who helps you get what's coming to him.

A lawyer is a person who prepares a 50,000-word document and calls it a brief.

A lawyer is an expert on justice in the same way a prostitute is an expert on love.

A lawyer will do anything to

win a case. Sometimes even tell
the truth.

If lawyers could be put on trial, they
would be accused of providing us with, but
not limited to herein, enough humorous ma-
terial to keep the world laughing until there
is no more income tax.

After listening to evidence by adverse
attorneys with restrictive provisions of di-
minished capacity, it is now safe to proclaim:

Whereas the American legal
system is an incredibly rich source
of humor; and

Whereas Americans are the
source of making lawyers incredibly rich; and

Whereas prosecutors, public
defenders, judges, jurors, and other
jesters of jurisprudence support the
economy by acquiring Mercedes,
Jaguars, BMWs and Hawaiian con-
dos; and

Whereas all these long-winded,
pompous professionals deserve to
be lampooned and poked fun at;

It is therefore, hereby consti-
tutionally certified by the California circuit court of comedy that
THE *Ultimate* LAWYERS JOKE

BOOK shall be adjudicated a legal, authorized, 100-percent kosher document guaranteed to elicit grins, giggles, and guffaws.

Case dismissed!

Larry Wilde
Chief of Justice of
Judicial Jesters

The minute you read something that you can't understand, you can almost be sure it was drawn up by a lawyer.

—WILL ROGERS

Legalese Laughs

Ezra and his nephew Jethro were sitting on the back porch of their Alabama farm house. "Why you like Moses so much?" asked Jethro.

"Moses was a great lawgiver," said Uncle Ezra. "But de way he was satisfied to keep de Ten Commandments short an' to de point shows he wasn't no regular lawyer."

*   *   *

A verbal contract isn't worth the paper it's written on.

—SAMUEL GOLDWYN

*   *   *

Says the layman to the milkman,
"Lemme have some cream."
Would a lawyer use such language?
Oh, no, he wouldn't dream
Of making it so easy
For the man to comprehend;
In asking for some cream or milk,
He would words and time expend.

"At your earliest convenience,"
The man of law would say,
Thereby meaning and intending
It be done without delay,
"A little lacteal fluid,
I need today, I find;
Will you please obtain the same for me,
If your cows are so inclined?"

*   *   *

Grocer: Oh, Doctor Barker, I hear lawyer
Ruthhaven is ill. How's he doing
now?
Doctor: Ah, poor fellow, he's lying at
death's door.
Grocer: That's nerve for you. At death's
door and still lying.

*   *   *

One morning, Ladonna dashed into a Detroit courtroom and said to the presiding judge, "Is you the judge of reprobate?"

"You're a little confused. I am the probate judge."

"Well, I guess this is the right place," said the black woman. "Mah husband was studyin' to be a preacher at a logical semitary and he died intesticled and left me three little infidels."

"Lady," said the judge, "the word is intestate, and I assume you also mean codicil."

"Ah guess so, judge. Ah just come to be appointed their executioner."

* * *

Terrill, who last year billed nine million dollars, was summoned to the office of the senior partner.

"You're behavior is despicable!" said the executive. "You've been badmouthing me to the press, you've been taking kickbacks from your staff, you've been embezzling money from the company, and now I learn you're having an affair with my wife. I'm warning you—one more thing and out you go!"

* * *

Hank Gordon, Florida's premier fishing boat captain, fractures clients with this cajoler:

Waltham, the senior partner of a large Louisville law firm, arrived at the Pearly Gates.

"What have you done that entitles you to admission?" asked St. Peter.

"I once gave a needy panhandler a dime."

"Gabriel, is that correct?"

"Yes, St. Peter."

"What else have you done?" requested St. Peter.

"Well, your Honor, that is, St. Peter, I once gave a newsboy a nickel."

"That's on the record book," said Gabriel.

"And what else have you done to your credit?"

"That's all I can think of now."

"Gabriel, what shall we do with this man?" asked St. Peter.

"Give him back his fifteen cents and tell him to go to Hell."

11

"Hey, what's the little boy crying about?"

"That big kid over there swiped his candy."

"But what's he crying about, you have the candy!"

"Yeah, I'm the little kid's lawyer."

*   *   *

If a friend were to give you an orange, he'd simply say, "Here's an orange."

But when the transaction is turned over to a legal practitioner, this is the way he puts it down:

"I hereby give and convey to you all and singular, my estate and interests, rights, title, claim, and advantages of and in said orange, together with all its rind, juice, pulp, pits, and all rights and advantages with full power to bite, cut, and otherwise eat the same or give the same away with and without the rind, skin, juice, pulp, or pits, anything herein before or herein after or in any other deed or deeds, instruments of whatever nature or kind whatsoever to the contrary in anywise notwithstanding."

Then a couple of smart Park Avenue lawyers come along and take it away from you.

*   *   *

What is the difference between an ordinary suit and a lawsuit?

The former gets cleaned and pressed for the client, while the latter is pressed while the client gets cleaned.

*   *   *

Miss Gibson said to her third grade class, "I'm going to ask each of you what your father does for a living. Bobby, you're first."

Bobby stood up and said, "My father runs the bank."

"Madeline?"

"My dad is a chef."

"Matthew?"

"My father plays piano in a whorehouse."

Miss Gibson changed the subject to arithmetic.

After school, the teacher went to Matthew's house and rang the bell. Matthew's father opened the door.

"Your son, Matthew, is in my class," said the teacher. "He says you play piano in a whorehouse for a living?"

"No," said the father. "Actually, I'm an attorney, but you can't tell *that* to an eight-year-old kid."

*   *   *

Some physicians direct their patients to lie always on the right side when asleep, declaring that it is injurious to the health to lie on both sides. Yet, lawyers as a group enjoy good health!

*   *   *   *

"Is he rich enough to keep an automobile and a yacht?"
"Yes, he is even richer than that. He's a lawyer."

*   *   *

In what way does a lawyer resemble a pelican?
In the length of his bill.

*   *   *

The man who said "talk is cheap" never hired a lawyer.

*   *   *

The lawyer was endeavoring to pump some free medical advice out of the doctor.
"Which side is it best to lie on, Doc?"
"The side that pays you the retainer."

*   *   *

The new law students gathered in the classroom for the first day's classes.

The law professor stared at them, wiped his glasses, and then spoke. "You are about to embark on a course of study that will try your very souls. Some of you will make it, and some of you will crack. A few of you will go on to bigger and better things. Those who crack will be lawyers."

*　　*　　*

BUMPER STICKER

Women Lawyers Make the Best Motions

*　　*　　*

Willoughby had been trying for months to collect a bill from a client, but all his letters and telegrams were completely disregarded. At last, being driven to devices short of the law, he sent a tear-jerking letter with a snapshot of his little daughter. The caption under the picture read, "The reason I must have the money you owe me."

He received an answer by mail and enclosed was a photo of a beautiful redhead in a bathing suit. The heading of his picture was, "The reason I can't pay."

*　　*　　*

Donald had a terrible sex life. No matter how hard he tried, he could not make out with a girl. One day his buddy, Rick, said, "I got the perfect babe for you. She loves to make it. But she likes to do it with anybody she thinks is important. Here's her phone number. Just tell her you're a big man in your field."

They met the next day. "Did you call her?" asked Rick.

"Yeah," replied Donald. "But she wouldn't go out with me."

"What'd you tell her?"

"I told her I was the sales manager of a big manufacturing company."

"No wonder she wouldn't go out with you," screamed Rick. "She likes professional men. Call her back tonight. Disguise your voice, and this time tell her you're a lawyer."

He phoned, told her he was an attorney, and they went out to dinner. They came back to her apartment and hopped right into bed. While they were making love Donald moaned, "How do you like this? I've only been an attorney for two hours and already I'm screwing somebody."

A successful Yuppie corporate attorney was explaining to a friend the five secrets of happiness: Money. Money. Money. Money. Money.

*   *   *

How many lawyers does it take to change a light bulb?

Fifty-two. Eight to argue, one to get a continuance, two to object, one to demur, two to research precedents, one to dictate a letter, one to stipulate, seven to turn in their time cards, one to depose, one to write interrogatories, two to settle, one to order a secretary to change the bulb, and twenty-six to bill for professional services.

*   *   *

Rabbi Gottesman met two members of his congregation at the home of a lawyer whom he considered too sharp a practitioner.

"Rabbi," asked the lawyer, "tell me something about these two members of your flock—do you look upon them as white sheep or black sheep?"

"I don't know," answered the rabbi, "whether they're black sheep or white, but I do know that if they stay here too long they're going to be fleeced."

*   *   *

A psychiatrist was giving his patient Nelson, a young Dallas divorce lawyer, a Rorschach test. The analyst was amazed to find that the Texan associated every ink blot with some bizarre sexual perversion.

"You'd better make another appointment," the shrink said when they finished. "You need a lot of help."

"Okay," said Nelson. "But right now I'm more concerned about mah date tonight. Ah wanna borrow those dirty pictures."

*   *   *

Closter was a little concerned about his pending court case. He asked his lawyer, "How should I plead?"

"On your knees," said the attorney.

*   *   *

One morning in a Jersey City elementary school, Miss Dressel asked her class, "Can you tell me the difference between 'unlawful' and 'illegal?' "

Little Tony raised his hand.

"All right," said Miss Dressel, "you may tell the class."

" 'Unlawful' is when you do somethin' the law don't allow," explained Tony, "and 'illegal' is a sick boid."

*   *   *

Benson and Gardner, two old prospectors from Colorado, quarreled and quarreled and finally landed before the local magistrate. Benson lost the case and shouted at his opponent, "I'll law you to the Circuit Court."

"Go ahead," said Gardner.

"An' I'll law you to the Supreme Court."

"I'll be there."

"An' I'll law you to hell," screeched the prospector.

"My attorney will be there," replied Gardner.

*   *   *

Dawley, the Yuppie Hollywood lawyer, stopped in front of a young man at a posh party.

"We've met before, haven't we?" he asked. "I never forget a face. We have met, haven't we?"

"Yes, sir," said the young man. "We've met before."

"Where was it?"

"In San Francisco, at that gay bar."

"Guess I got the wrong man," said the lawyer, "but there's quite a resemblance."

*   *   *

20

What do you have when you have one lawyer in a town?

Too little work.

What do you have when you have two lawyers in a town?

Too much work.

*   *   *

Jim Barton, the magnificent Milligan News Agency bookseller, breaks up school buyers with this beaut:

A crochety dean of the law department at a New England university answered the phone, "All right," he snapped, "what do you want?"

"Is this the city gas works?" asked the voice at the other end.

"No, it is not!" exclaimed the dean. "This happens to be the university law school."

"Well," said the woman, "I didn't miss it by much, did I?"

*   *   *

APPEAL

What a client usually does
if he has any money left.

*   *   *

Julie Wildman, the cute clinical psychologist, cracks up patients with this pearl:

Silverman and his wife were watching their four-year-old daughter Rhoda playing along the water's edge at Miami Beach.

"You know, you're in court all day shouting at witnesses, objecting to the judge," she said. "Sometimes I think you're too strict with Rhoda."

"That's ridiculous," said the trial lawyer.

Just then the little girl ran into the surf. Silverman jumped up and shouted, "Rhoda! Stop that! You're tracking sand into the ocean."

A wholesaler in New York sent a letter to the postmaster of a small Tennessee town. He asked for the name of some honest lawyer who would take a collection case against a local debtor who had refused to pay for a shipment of the wholesaler's goods. He got this reply:

Dear Sir:
I am the postmaster of this village and received your letter. I am also an honest lawyer and ordinarily would be pleased to accept a case against a local debtor. In this case, however, I also happen to be the person you sold those crummy goods to. I received your demand to pay and refused to honor it. I am also the banker you sent the draft to draw on the merchant, and I sent that back with a note stating that the merchant had refused to pay. And if I were not, for the time being, substituting for the pastor of our local church, I would tell you just where to stick your claim.

* * *

CASE

Something you pay your attorney to have the courts postpone from time to time until nobody cares whether it is actually decided or not.

* * *

A professor of a mid-west law school was dismissing his class for the Christmas holidays:

"Remember boys, if you have sexual intercourse with a young lady who is under age but with her consent, it is statutory rape. If you have sexual intercourse with a young lady who is of age but without her consent, it is rape. But if you have sexual intercourse with a young lady who is of age and with her consent, then I wish you a Merry Christmas. But I warn you, there are still some risks involved even though it is not rape."

* * *

"And what do you do, sir?"
"I'm a criminal lawyer."
"Aren't they all!"

* * *

The penalty for laughing in a court-room is six months in jail—if it weren't for this penalty, the jury would never hear the evidence.

—BOB HOPE

*   *   *

Did you hear about the process server in Oklahoma City who's getting altogether too cocky to suit his cronies?

They don't like the way he's been putting on the writs.

*   *   *

Shellie Evans, WESTAMERICA's banking wizard, wins customers with this wisp of waggery:

Brizzolaria and Strobenfenster, two Cleveland attorneys, decided that they had attained a position in the community which demanded they change their names to something simpler. So the firm's name became Booker and Booker.

One morning the receptionist received this call, "Hello, I'd like to speak to Mr. Booker, please."

"Sir," she asked, "which Mr. Booker would you like to talk to, Mr. Brizzolaria or Mr. Strobenfenster?"

*   *   *

COURTROOM CACKLES

The plaintiff's attorney was questioning the witness: "What is your occupation?"

"I'm a bricklayer," answered the witness.

"Ha, a mere bricklayer, eh?" sneered the lawyer. "What do you think your position is in society?"

"Well, mister, I realize being a bricklayer ain't the most distinguished occupation in the world, but I feel I've done better than my father."

"And what was your father?" snapped the lawyer.

"A shyster lawyer!"

*   *   *

Lawyer: Do you know what a conscience is?

Witness: Sure I do.

Lawyer: Well, what is it?

Witness: Well, my parents wanted me to be a lawyer, but I've got a conscience.

*   *   *

COURT

Often referred to as a place where they dispense with justice.

*   *   *

A newly qualified judge in Louisiana was trying his first criminal case. Crawford, the prisoner before him, had appeared in court before on a similar charge and was then acquitted.

"Well," said the judge, "according to these records I see you're in the same kind of trouble."

"Yessir," said Crawford, "the last time yawl was mah lawyer, 'member?"

"Yes, I remember. Where is your lawyer this time?"

"Well, ya Honor, ah ain't got no lawyer this time. This time ahm gonna tell the truth."

*   *   *

"You have known the defendant how long?"

"Fourteen years."

"Tell the court whether or not you think he is the type of man who would steal this money."

"How much was it?"

*   *   *

"You seem to have more than the average share of intelligence for a man of your background," sneered the lawyer at a witness on the stand.

"If I wasn't under oath, I'd return the compliment," replied the witness.

*   *   *

During a cross-examination of the witness, the counsel asked, "Now tell the court your name."

"Eisenhower," replied the witness.

"And your first name?"

"Dwight."

"Dwight Eisenhower, eh?" remarked the attorney. "That's a fairly well-known name."

"It ought to be," he replied. "I've worked in this town for the past twenty-five years."

*   *   *

Boitano appeared as a witness in a suit. The attorney asked, "Where were you on the night of July 10?"

"Your Honor, I object," yelled the counsel for the defense.

"That's all right, go ahead ask me," said Boitano. The prosecutor repeated the question and again the defense objected.

"Hey. Why shouldn't he ask me?" said Boitano. "I'll answer."

The judge said, "If the witness insists on answering, there is no reason for the defense to object." So the attorney again repeated the question, "Where were you on the night of July 10?"

Boitano said, "I don't know."

*   *   *

Old Berkson had witnessed a crime, and the lawyer said to him, "Describe to the jury just how the stairs run in that house."

The elderly Swede looked dazed and scratched his head for a minute before attempting a reply. "You vant to know how de stairs run?" he repeated.

"Yes, if you please, how the stairs run."

"Vell," said Berkson slowly, "ven aye bane oopstairs day run down, and ven aye bane downstairs dey run oop."

*   *   *

Judge: Have you ever been in trouble before?

Defendant: Your Honor, all I did was to rob my kid brother's bank.

D.A.: Your Honor, the defendant forgot to explain that his kid brother was treasurer of the First National Bank.

* * *

A crochety old resident of Sun City was bitten by a dog, and he contended that it was his neighbor's canine. When the neighbor was brought to court, he offered this defense: "Your Honor, first of all let me tell you my dog wouldn't do such a thing. Second, he is blind and can't see to bite anyone. Third, even if he could see, he couldn't stumble over to bite anyone on account of his lameness. Fourth, he has no teeth. And fifth, my dog died six weeks ago. Lastly, I never had a dog."

* * *

COURT

A place where the wealthy go for protection.

* * *

Gonzales was sworn in and Judge Andrea Barnard instructed him, "Now speak to the jury, the people sitting behind you on the benches."

The Mexican stood up, bowed, and said, "*Buenos dias,* ladies and gentlemen."

33

Feinberg, an elderly Jewish shopkeeper, was on the witness stand.

"And sir, how old are you?" asked the attorney for the state.

"I am *kaynahora*,* seventy-eight."

"What?"

"I said I am *kaynahora*, seventy-eight."

"Just answer the question, please. Without comments. Now then, how old are you?"

"*Kaynahora*, seventy-eight."

The judge intervened: "You will answer the question, and only the question, or I shall hold you in contempt of court!"

The counsel for the defense cleared his throat. "If it please the court, may I be permitted to ask the question?" He turned to the old man. "*Kaynahora*, how old are you?"

The old man said, "Seventy-eight."

*Jewish term (superstitious) to protect one from evil, like "knock wood."

*   *   *

Chang Yee returned to Shanghai and described a trial in English law courts: "One man is quite silent, another talks all the time, and twelve men ignore the talkative man and condemn the man who has not said a word."

*   *   *

The judge said, "Mr. Tannenbaum, you are a key witness. You must tell us only what you actually saw. You must not give hearsay evidence. Is that perfectly clear?"

"Yes, sir."

The prosecuting attorney asked, "What is your name?"

"Morris L. Tannenbaum."

"How old are you?"

"That depends on when I was born. And that I can't tell you, even though I was there. Hearsay evidence, that's all I have."

* * *

Judge: What's the charge, officer?
Cop: Fragrancy, your Honor. He's been drinking perfume.

* * *

Umbach, charged with embezzlement, appeared in court without counsel.

"How is it you don't have a lawyer?" asked Judge Margaret Olivera.

"Well, I did hire an attorney," explained the suspect, "but as soon as he found out that I didn't steal the fifty thousand dollars, he wouldn't have nothing to do with my case."

* * *

Immigrant Salvatelli was called to give evidence in a trial involving a shooting.

"Did you or did you not see the shot fired?" began the magistrate.

"I no see it, but I'm-a tellin' you I heard."

"That is not satisfactory. Step down."

As the Italian turned to go, he laughed, and was immediately rebuked by the magistrate.

"Hey, you Honna, did you-a see me laugh?"

"No, but I heard you."

"Atsa no satisfactory."

* * *

The lawsuit was in full swing, wherein the plaintiffs, Maria and Jesse Ortiz, were suing a trucking company as a result of a traffic accident.

"Mrs. Ortiz, you say the collision threw you and your husband across the street and that your husband suffered a fractured skull and a broken arm. Now, tell us what happened to you. Did you get hurt in the fracas?"

"Not exactly. Actually, it was a little higher up."

* * *

Judge: What is your name?
Witness: Abraham Liebowitz.
Judge: Are you married?
Witness: Of coss!
Judge: Whom did you marry?
Witness: Vot else? A voman.
Judge: Mr. Liebowitz, didn't you ever hear of anyone marrying anybody else but a woman?
Witness: You sad it. Mine sister, she married a man.

*   *   *

RETAINER

The first holdup.

*   *   *

The South Carolina judge looked at Jeeter when he took the witness stand and said, "Do you understand what you are to swear to?"

"Yes, sah, ah onderstands. Ah am to sweah and tell de truf."

"That's right," continued the magistrate, "and what will happen if you do not tell the truth? Do you know?"

"Well, yo Honah," said the black, "ah 'spects ouah side'll win de case."

*   *   *

Twelve-year-old Angelo was accused of fathering a child. He stood before the judge with his attorney. The lawyer, in order to prove the ridiculousness of the charge, unzipped the boy's pants.

"Your honor," said the lawyer, "look at this tiny organ, this immature equipment. How could a boy father a baby with this little, undeveloped—"

"Hey, mista," whispered Angelo, "you betta quit strokin' me like that or we're gonna lose this case!"

*   *   *

Old Barlow was a crossing-tender at a junction where an express train demolished an automobile and its occupants. Being the chief witness, his testimony was vitally important. Barlow explained that the night was dark, and he had waved his lantern frantically, but the driver of the car paid no attention to the signal.

The railroad company won the case, and the president of the company complimented the old-timer for his story. "You did wonderfully," he said, "I was afraid you would waver in your testimony."

"No sir," exclaimed the senior, "but I sure was afraid that the durned lawyer was gonna ask me if my lantern was lit."

*   *   *

McQuillan was on the stand. The case involved a railroad and several of the passengers who were injured.

"You say," thundered the counsel for the railroad, "that you saw the two trains crash head-on while doing sixty miles an hour. What did you say when you saw this happen?"

"I said to meself," replied the Irishman, "this is a helluva way to run a railroad."

*　　*　　*

Judge: If I let you off this time, will you, Shamus O'Shea, promise this court to take the pledge?

Prisoner: I'd be delighted to, your Honor. And I'll drink to your health for doing this for me.

*　　*　　*

"And now, Mrs. O'Reilly," said the lawyer, "will you be kind enough to tell the court whether your husband was in the habit of striking you with impunity?"

"With what, sir?"

"With impunity."

"He was, now that I think of it, but more often he struck me with his bare fists."

*　　*　　*

Alan Brookes, the popular Cincinnati schoolmaster, stimulates students with this smile-grabber:

Three little boys, Russell, Alex and Warren, raided the apple orchard of a farm and were caught. They were brought before a kindly judge. He asked them who their fathers were and what they would do to keep out of further difficulties.

Russell said, "I've learned my lesson. My father is a doctor and he says green apples will make me sick."

Alex replied, "I'm real sorry. I'm a banker's son and stealing apples is not in keeping with my family's reputation."

Then Warren said, "I won't do it again. But my father is a lawyer and I'm gonna sue that farmer for damages, 'cause I tore my clothes on his tree."

Balducci was brought into court charged with beating his wife. The judge delivered a long lecture and concluded with, "If your wife brings you here again, I'll send you to jail."

A few weeks later he was back in court.

"What did I tell you?" charged the magistrate.

"Just a minute, you Honor. It was-a like this. We was-a sittin' on the back-a stoop and mama said, 'you only behave-a 'cause you afraid of that no-good bum-a judge.' You Honor, when she say that 'bout you, I just-a pull back and smack her in-a da mouth."

* * *

Old Viggiani was under indictment for a minor traffic offense and was without counsel representation. The judge appointed a lawyer to defend the elderly Italian. However, it was obvious to all that the young lawyer had never tried a case in court. As he eagerly walked forward to consult his first client, Viggiani turned to the judge and said, "Yo Honah, is dis da man atsa gonna offend me?"

"Yes."

"In that-a case," continued the defendant, "I'm-a gonna plead guilty."

* * *

Robert Holmes, the award-winning California sculptor, regales Irish clients with this shenanigan:

The case concerned a will and Kelley was the witness.

"Was the deceased," asked the attorney, "in the habit of talking to himself when he was alone?"

"I don't know," said the Irishman.

"Come now man, you don't know and yet you pretend you were intimately acquainted with the deceased?"

"Well, Mr. Lawyer," said Kelley, "I never happened to be with him when he was alone."

*   *   *

Judge: (to the Irish immigrant) Why did you assault and throw this man on the floor when he was serving your meal?

Defendant: Yer Honor, yer see Moike, that's me boy, tole me befoore oi left home, 'Don't yez ferget to tip the waiter.' So oi did!

*   *   *

There are two kinds of lawyers—those who know the law and those who know the judge.

Three streetwalkers were in a New York City night court, as well as Finkleman, an old Jewish peddler, arrested for selling panty hose on Lexington Avenue without a license.

"This is all a mistake, your Honor," said the first hooker. "I was walkin' along and this guy—"

"Just a minute, young lady," said the judge. "You've been here a dozen times. One hundred dollars fine. Next!"

"I'm just a poor, private secretary," said the second girl, "and I wasn't doin' nothin'—"

"I recognize you too, miss," said the magistrate. "Two hundred dollars or ten days in jail. Next case!"

"Judge," said the third girl, "I'm a prostitute! I'm not proud of it, but it's the only way I can support my three kids. I'm guilty!"

"Young woman," said the judge, "I like your honesty. And because of it, I'm going to give you a break. Your case is dismissed. And sergeant, give this girl fifty dollars out of the Policemen's Fund!"

Now comes Finkelman, the old Jewish peddler, arrested for selling panty hose without a license. "Your Honor," he pleaded, "I'm not gonna lie to you. I'm a prostitute!"

*   *   *

Judicial Jests

A news reporter sat before Judge Cameron in his spacious chambers conducting an interview.

"You seem to make more decisions than any of the other judges," said the newsman. "How do you do it?"

"I hear the plaintiff and render my decision."

"Don't you listen to the defendants?"

"I used to, but I found it confused me."

*　　*　　*

"Are all the newsreel cameramen here, Bailiff?"

"Yes, your Honor."

"Lights set?"

"Yes, they are."

"Sound checked?"

"Sound is all right."

"Good. Then let justice take its course."

* * *

JUDGE

The official representative
of the law's delays

* * *

Witness: Your Honor, that man is a dirty, mean, nasty scoundrel. And furthermore . . .

Judge: Silence!

Witness: But your Honor, I know the truth.

Judge: That will be enough. We don't want any of that here.

* * *

What has eighteen legs and a vagina?
The Supreme Court.

* * *

Old Mrs. Stockley climbed onto the witness stand, sat down, and the prosecuting attorney began his questioning.

"Do you know me?" he asked.

"I've lived in this town all my life, and I know just about everyone who's ever lived here. I remember you from nursery school, and all I can say is that you're a crook!"

Taken aback, the attorney asked, "Well, do you know the opposing attorney?"

"I certainly do. Known him since he was knee-high, and he's a crook too."

The judge called the attorney to the bench and whispered in his ear, "If you ask her if she knows me, I'll charge you with contempt!"

*   *   *

Patrice, an elderly prostitute, stood before newly elected Judge Cordell. Her appeal for leniency was so convincing that Cordell had doubts about sentencing her. He called a short recess, then went to the chambers of an older judge. "Say, Butler," he asked, "what would you give a sixty-year-old prostitute?"

"Oh," said the learned jurist, "no more than six dollars."

*   *   *

A pickpocket was brought before a Milwaukee magistrate for the obvious crime of picking pockets. The judge lectured him for several hours and finally fined the culprit one hundred dollars.

"But, your Honor," said the prisoner, "I only got sixty dollars!"

"Hm," said the judge, "in that case, guard, allow the prisoner to circulate around the courtroom. He should be able to raise the other forty dollars."

Prosecutor: Your Honor, the sheriff's cocker spaniel has gone and chewed up the court Bible.

Judge: Well, make the witness kiss the cocker spaniel, then. We can't adjourn court just to hunt up a new Bible.

*   *   *

Justice in the old west was administered in a simple manner, often by men who were not trained in the law. Here is a case presided over by the notorious Judge Roy Bean:

"Gentlemen, I have here before me a check, which some might call a bribe, from the plaintiff for fifteen thousand dollars, and I also have another check for ten thousand dollars from the defendant in the case. Now I propose to return five thousand dollars to the plaintiff, and then I'll be able to decide the case strictly on its merits."

*   *   *

Did you hear about the two gay judges that tried each other?

*   *   *

Bob Murphey, the superb Texas yarn spinner, gets screams with this tall tale:

Witness Farrell was asked to tell what he found on the premises.

"Naught but barren nothingness, as Shakespeare says," testified Farrell.

"Never mind what Shakespeare says!" snapped Judge Estrada. "If he knows anything about this case, he can be summoned!"

*   *   *

At one of the judicial conferences years ago, a newly appointed judge met the great federal judge, Learned Hand. "Since I've just been appointed, do you have any suggestions for me?"

"Judge, I will give you this bit of advice."

"Yes, sir?"

"Never," said Judge Hand, "go on the bench without first taking a piss."

*   *   *

"You are lying so clumsily," said the judge to the defendant, "that I would advise you to get a lawyer."

*   *   *

Judge Colerain was deaf. He was hearing a case in which both plaintiff and defendant also were deaf.

"This man ought to be made to pay his rent," said the deaf plaintiff.

"What have you got to say about that?" asked Colerain.

"Well," said the deaf defendant, "I always grind my corn by night."

Finally the deaf judge said, "I have considered this case carefully and have reach the decision that both of these brothers should help to support their mother."

*　　*　　*

A circuit judge traveling through a small New Mexico town in 1887 was asked to try a divorce case that involved a lot of sexy testimony. When the judge entered the courtroom, he noticed that it was crowded with women. He looked them over and said, "Guess folks here don't know the kind of case we're going to try. Therefore, I feel I ought to ask all the respectable women to withdraw."

Not one of them made a move.

"All right," the judge continued, "now that all the respectable women have gone, I order the bailiff to put the others out."

*　　*　　*

52

Reynolds was hauled into court for speeding and reckless driving. After a lengthy sermon by Judge Simpson, Reynolds quipped, "My, aren't you the eloquent one? I'll bet you can recite Lincoln's Gettysburg Address, too."

"I'm proud to say I can," admitted the black judge. "And I hereby sentence you to four-score and seven days in jail."

*   *   *

Judge Friedman was about to sentence a sixty-year-old prisoner:

Friedman: I hereby sentence you to thirty years penal servitude.

Prisoner: (sobbing) Your Honor, I won't live long enough to serve the sentence.

Friedman: It's all right. Just do what you can.

*   *   *

A defendant appeared before Laura Ling Chen, a Los Angeles jurist, and, hoping for lenience, pleaded, "Judge, I'm down and out."

The judge said, "You're down, but you are not out. Six months."

*   *   *

Martin Budd, the brilliant Connecticut barrister treats buddies to this nifty nugget:

The people of San Diego held a banquet for the town's favorite jurist. This judge, though illustrious, was exceedingly long-winded.

His after-dinner remarks to the gathering had been in progress for about two hours, and still he was not through. Then he said, "My friends, I speak not only for today, but for those who will come after us!"

A voice called out: "But it's not necessary to talk 'til they get here!"

A debtor on the witness stand cried, "As God is my judge, I do not owe the money."

The judge replied: "He is not. I am. You do."

* * *

"Fine advice you gave me! You said if I were friendly with the Judge, he'd let me off easy."

"Well, didn't he let you off easy?"

"No. I walked in to court and said, 'Hi, your Honor—how's the old kid today?' and he said, 'Fine—fifty dollars.' "

* * *

Escobar, a southern California magistrate, had just ruled on a case, and an attorney for the defense jumped to his feet and questioned the judge's decision.

"I can't reopen the case after I've given my decision," said Judge Escobar.

The lawyer replied, "Well, I guess I may as well leave, your Honor. There's no use knocking my head against a stone wall."

"I agree," said the judge. "But I don't know anyone who could do it with less personal injury than yourself."

* * *

Judge: You are charged with throwing your mother-in-law out of your fourth-story window.

Defendant: I did it without thinking, your Honor.

Judge: Yes, but don't you see how dangerous it might have been for anyone passing at the time?

*   *   *

"I know I can prove conclusively that I am innocent," said the defendant. "All I need is time."

"Nine months," said the Judge.

*   *   *

From the bench said the senile Judge Percival,
"Young man, counsel claims you'll get worse if I'll
          Send you to jail
        So I'll put you on bail."
Now wasn't Judge Percival merciful?

*   *   *

A New Hampshire judge received this card from a prison inmate, "Serving some wonderful time. Wish you were here."

*   *   *

Two Tennessee farmers were arguing over which smelled the stronger, a goat or a hobo. Finally after much ado they agreed to leave it to the county judge. "All right," said the judge, "bring in your subjects."

They brought in the goat and the judge fainted. Then they brought in the tramp, and the goat fainted.

Magistrate: What is the defendant charged with?

Bailiff: He is a camera fiend, your Honor.

Magistrate: But he shouldn't have been arrested just because he has a mania for taking pictures.

Bailiff: It isn't that, sir, he takes the cameras.

*   *   *

The legendary Judge Brandeis was once asked to settle a family dispute. Two brothers were fighting over the fair division of a large estate left them by their father.

His decision was classic:

"Let one brother divide the estate, and let the other brother have first choice."

*   *   *

A judge and a bishop were arguing about their relative authority. "I'm afraid there isn't much room for debate," said the bishop. "After all, you can only say, 'You be hanged,' whereas I have the power to say, 'You be damned!' "

"Very true," said the jurist. "But when a judge says to a man, 'You be hanged,' he is hanged."

*   *   *

"What were you doing about that chicken coop at midnight, Cleophus?" the judge asked.

"Jes' circulatin' roun', jedge, jes' circulatin' roun'."

"Clerk, make a notation: 'Withdrawn from circulation for sixty days.' "

* * *

"Silence in the courtroom!" shouted the North Carolina judge. "Half a dozen men have been tried and convicted and sentenced already without the court's having been able to hear a word of the testimony."

* * *

Defendant: It is difficult to see how I can be a forger. Why, I can't sign my own name.

Judge: You are not charged with signing your own name.

* * *

"You are accused of stealing a chicken. Have you anything to say about it?"

"I took it for a lark."

"No resemblance whatsoever. Thirty days."

* * *

A sharp Baltimore barrister was pleading his case. "My client stole the ring only in a moment of weakness."

"I suppose," said Judge Melissa Kwan Tung, "if he'd had a moment of strength, he would have taken a safe."

*   *   *

McQuillan was brought before the court and charged with intoxication. "Where did you get that liquor?" asked Judge Jefferson.

"A Scotsman gave it to me, your Honor," said the Irishman.

"Twenty-five dollars for perjury," charged his Honor.

*   *   *

In a small Missouri community, an old horse doctor was elected justice of the peace, and what he didn't know about the law could fill a library. His first case was a man arrested for stealing a horse.

"Guilty or not guilty?" asked the justice.

"Not guilty," answered the defendant.

"Then what the devil are you doing here?" shouted the justice. "Get out!"

*   *   *

Judge:	What is this man charged with?
Bailiff:	Intoxication, your Honor.
Judge:	Drunk, eh?
Prisoner:	Judge, I'm as sober as you are this minute.
Judge:	Pleads guilty, twenty-five days. Next case!

*　　*　　*

"No, your Honor," said Hennessy. "I was certainly not drunk, though I may have been intoxicated."

"Well," said the magistrate, "I intended to fine you one hundred dollars, but in view of your explanation, I make it a *C* note."

*　　*　　*

Breitholle and Ganson before a probate judge got involved in an argument. Breitholle, losing his self-control, exclaimed, "You are the biggest jackass I have ever had the misfortune to set my eyes upon in a court of law."

"Order! Order!" said the judge. "You seem to forget that I am in the room."

*　　*　　*

It ain't no sin if you crack a
few laws now and then, just so
long as you don't break any.
                    —MAE WEST

                *   *   *

"Never judge a woman by her clothes,"
advised a most observing magistrate. "There
isn't enough evidence."

                *   *   *

A West Virginia back country judge,
before passing sentence, would look in a
book resembling a law book that actually
was a Sears Roebuck catalogue.

One day he said to a prisoner, "For
being drunk and disorderly, you are fined
$49.98 and two days on the road gang."

As the man was being led from the
courtroom, he said to the sheriff, "He sure
was tough on me."

"You were lucky," said the sheriff.
"If he'd opened that book to the plumbing
section instead of the pants section, you
might've been workin' on the roads for life."

Defendant Ditties

The presiding judge had just completed rendering the court's verdict and was about to pass sentence when he asked the defendant if he had anything to say.

"No, judge, there is nothing I care to say," answered the prisoner. "But if you'll clear away the tables and chairs in this here courtroom for me to beat the hell outa that no-good lawyer of mine, you can give me a year or two extra."

*   *   *

A burly prisoner from New York's East Side stood before the judge and jury. It was obvious this was his first time in a court. The court clerk asked, "Prisoner at the bar, do you wish to challenge any of the jury?"

"Well, I'm not in the best of condition," said the defendant, "but I think I can stand a couple of rounds with that fat old fart in the front row."

Thompkins was cross-examining the defendant.

"After you poisoned the coffee, your husband sat at the breakfast table with you and sipped it. Didn't you feel the slightest pity for him?"

"Yes," she answered. "There was a moment when I felt sorry for him."

"When was that?" inquired the lawyer.

"When he asked for a second cup."

*   *   *

Lawyer: Where were you on the evening of August 10?
Defendant: I believe I was with a couple of friends of mine.
Lawyer: Scoundrels and cheats, probably.
Defendant: I think you're right. Both of them were lawyers.

*   *   *

Judge: This is a serious charge, Armstrong. You want me to appoint a lawyer to defend you?
Prisoner: Naw, judge, thanks. Every time I had a lawyer, they locked me up and let the lawyer go free. This time, judge, I'm gonna throw myself on the ignorance of the court.

*   *   *

68

Before the start of court proceedings, the magistrate advised the defendant, "Remember, anything you say will be held against you."

"Really?" replied the prisoner.

"Yes," continued the judge. "Now, what have you to say?"

"Racquel Welch."

*   *   *

Old Mrs. Rothstein was being cross-examined by a lawyer who was not too subtle in his approach.

At the conclusion of the cross-examination, the barrister said, "You say you had no education, but you answered my questions smartly enough."

She replied, "You don't have to be no scholar to answer such silly questions."

*   *   *

Judge to defendant: "Colonel Calhoun, why are you called 'Colonel?' I don't think you were ever in the army. What regiment were you in?"

"Well, suh, it's like this. The 'Colonel' in front of my name is like when someone calls you the 'Honorable' Judge Womack. It don't mean a thing!"

*   *   *

"You told this court that you met the defendant on a bus and that he had been drinking and gambling?" charged the counsel for the defendant.

"That's true."

"Now tell the court, did you see him take a drink?"

"Well, no, I didn't."

"Aha," said the attorney, "did you see the defendant gambling?"

"No."

"Then, how can you tell this court that the defendant had been drinking and gambling?"

"Well," explained the witness, "he gave the bus driver a blue chip for his carfare and told him to keep the chaser."

*   *   *

"You do not have a lawyer?" asked the court.

"No," replied the prisoner.

"Then," said the judge, "I'll appoint one to defend you."

"Please," said the prisoner, "if it's all the same to you, judge, just give me an interpreter to tell me what you're talking about."

*   *   *

"And how do you plead?"

"I plead guilty and waive the hearing."

"What do you mean, 'waive the hearing?'"

"I mean I don't wanna hear no more about it."

*   *   *

Isabel McNally approached the jury box and began an eloquent plea for her client:

"Ladies and gentlemen of the jury, I want to tell you about this man. There is so much to say that is good: He never beat his mother; he was always kind to little children; he never did a dishonest thing in his life; he has always lived by the golden rule; he is a model of everything decent, forthright, and honest. Everyone loves him and . . ."

Her client leaned over to a friend and said, "How do ya like dat babe? I pay her good dough to defend me, and she's tellin' the jury about some other guy."

*   *   *

We the jury find the defendant innocent and his lawyer guilty.

*   *   *

71

Ross Hersey, king of the shaggy dog stories, kills crowds with this corker:

Shantz was defending a man charged with housebreaking. Addressing the court he said, "Your Honor, I contend that my client did not break into the house. The living room window was open, and he simply inserted his right arm and removed several articles. Actually, the crime was committed by a part of his body, and you cannot punish the whole for a crime committed by the part."

The judge said, "Your argument has some logic, hence I sentence the prisoner's arm to five years imprisonment. He can accompany it or not, as he chooses."

So with the lawyer's help, the defendant unscrewed his artificial arm and walked out of the courtroom.

Judge: You again! On another drunk charge! Hampton, didn't I tell you I didn't want to see you here again?

Hampton: Yes, suh! Dat's what I tried to tell these policemen, but they wouldn't believe me.

* * *

The United States may have the only judicial system in the world where they lock up the jury at night and let the defendant go home.

* * *

"You've committed six burglaries in a week," said Judge Siracusa.

"That's right," replied the defendant. "If everyone worked as hard as I do, we'd be on the road to prosperity."

* * *

"How could you swindle people who trusted in you?" asked the judge.

"But your Honor," said the defendant, "people who don't trust in you cannot be swindled."

* * *

A client between two lawyers is like a fish between two cats.

*   *   *

Krause was flabbergasted to learn that his client had sent a case of scotch to the judge.

"Good heavens man, you're sure to lose your case now."

"Oh, no, I'll win it," said the defendant. "I sent it in my opponent's name."

*   *   *

"You told me how good you were when I hired you three weeks ago," said Ronzini to his lawyer.

"That's true," said the attorney.

"Would you mind tellin' me all over again!" said the defendant. "I'm gettin' discouraged."

*   *   *

"Why did you throw the pot of geraniums at the plaintiff?"

"Because of an advertisement, your Honor."

"What advertisement?"

" 'Say it with flowers.' "

*   *   *

Judge:	Give your name, occupation, and the charge against you.
Prisoner:	My name is Sparks. I'm an electrician and the charge is battery.
Judge:	All right, officer, put him in a dry cell.
Prisoner:	This is a terrible shock.

*　　*　　*

At the preliminary hearing Judge Dixon stared at the hardened criminal. "Because of the gravity of this case," he said, "I am going to give you three lawyers."

"Never mind, your Honor," replied the defendant. "Just get me one good witness."

*　　*　　*

The jury had returned a verdict of guilty, and the judge was about to sentence the prisoner.

"You have been convicted on twenty-six counts, and you are hereby committed by the power of this court to the state prison for a cumulative sentence of ninety-nine years. What have you to say?"

"Nothing, your Honor," replied the prisoner, "except ain't you pretty free with another man's time?"

*　　*　　*

"You stole eggs from this man's store," said the judge. "Have you any excuse?"

"Yes, I took them by mistake," said the defendant.

"How is that?"

"I thought they were fresh."

*   *   *

A man had been convicted on circumstantial evidence. The conviction made him a violator of the habitual criminal statute, which carries a sentence of life imprisonment. In proving the prisoner's previous convictions, his record was placed before the court by the prosecutor. It revealed the man had been in prison at the time of the commission of the crime for which he had last been convicted.

"Good heavens, man!" exclaimed his attorney. "Why didn't you tell us this?"

"I thought it might prejudice the jury against me," he replied.

*   *   *

Judge: Why did you stick your knife in this man?

Prisoner: Well, I heard the police coming and I had to hide it somewhere and he was real convenient.

*   *   *

Rodriguez was charged with breaking and entering and robbery. The case having been presented to the court by the city prosecutor, he was ordered to stand up.

"Have you a lawyer?" asked the court.

"No, sir."

"Are you able to employ one?"

"No, sir."

"Do you want a lawyer to defend the case?"

"Not really, sir."

"Well, what do you propose to do about the case?"

"Well," said the defendant, "Far's I'm concerned, I'm willin' to drop the case."

*   *   *

"This charge of perjury against you is very serious," said Krantz to his client. "The word 'perjury' means . . . well, what does a cat do when it licks up its milk? Purr."

"That's right," said the defendant. "They purr."

"Now what do they call twelve men who decide the fate of a criminal?"

"A jury."

"Correct. Now put them together and what have you got?"

"Twelve men who lap up cat's milk?"

*   *   *

"All right, Mr. Bateman," said attorney Charlotte Parks to her new client, "I'll take the case. I feel assured that I can get you justice."

"For goodness sakes," replied Bateman, "if that's the best you can do I'd better get another lawyer."

*   *   *

Judge: I notice that in addition to stealing this money, you took a lot of valuable jewelry.
Prisoner: Yes, your Honor. You see, I was always taught that money alone does not bring happiness.

*   *   *

Kim Wah Low went to his lawyer to collect the fire insurance settlement on his store. The merchant was shocked to discover how much the attorney was keeping in fees.

"The case has been in litigation a long time," explained the attorney. "I've earned it."

"Holy Confucius," muttered the client, "you'd think *you* started the fire."

*   *   *

Carlson was charged with stealing a Mercedes Benz, and after a long trial, the jury acquitted him. Later that day Carlson came back to the judge who had presided at the hearing.

"Your Honor," he said, "I wanna get out a warrant for that dirty lawyer of mine."

"Why?" asked the judge. "He won your acquittal. What do you want to have him arrested for?"

"Well, your Honor," replied Carlson, "I didn't have the money to pay his fee, so he went and took the car I stole."

"Judge," cried the prisoner at the bar, "have I got to be tried by an all-lady jury?"

"Be quiet," whispered his attorney.

"I won't be quiet. Judge, I can't even fool my own wife, let alone twelve strange women. I'm guilty."

*   *   *

Judge: Turner, is your wife dependent upon you?

Turner: She sho is, judge. If I didn't go out and get the washin' and bring it home for her to do, she'd starve to death.

*   *   *

A stock broker said to Schacter, "If you win this case for me, I'll pay you ten thousand dollars."

"Okay," said the lawyer. "Get me some witnesses."

The broker produced the witnesses, and Shacter won the case for him. When the verdict was in, the lawyer said, "I'll expect a check for ten thousand dollars from you, as you promised."

And the client replied, "Get me some witnesses."

*   *   *

"Why did you steal the pearl necklace from the jeweler's shop window?" asked the judge.

"Because," said the defendant, "it had on it 'this beautiful string of pearls could be yours,' and I couldn't resist it!"

* * *

The judge wanted to make sure that the defendant understood the importance of what he'd done.

"Do you know what that oath you have just taken means?" the judge asked.

"Yeah," answered the witness. "It means if I swear to a lie, I gotta stick to it."

* * *

Lila Wulff, San Francisco's stunning theater exec, savors this lulu:

A Bel Air lawyer was visited by a beautiful young starlet who tried to engage his services for a seduction suit against her neighbor. "You don't have sufficient facts to support such a case," said the attorney.

Downcast and disappointed she left the office. The following day she returned and reported, "I think we've got him. He seduced me again last night."

* * *

Judge: (about to commit for trial) You certainly effected the robbery in a remarkably proficient way; in fact, with outstanding cunning—

Prisoner: Now, now, your Honor, no flattery please. You'll make me self-conscious.

* * *

The pompous judge glared over his desk at the tattered prisoner who had been dragged before the court on a charge of vagrancy.

"Have you ever earned an honest dollar in your life, you good-for-nothing drifter?"

"Yes, your Honor," was the answer. "I voted for you in the last election."

* * *

"Lemuel, do you solemnly swear to tell the truth, the whole truth, and nothing but the truth, so help you God?"

"I do, sir."

"Well, now Lemuel, what have you got to say for yourself?"

"Judge, with all them limitations you just put on me, I don't believe I have anything at all to say."

* * *

84

OVERHEARD AT A MANHATTAN NIGHT COURT BETWEEN THE JUDGE AND THE DEFENDANT:

"That'll be twenty dollars or twenty days."

"I'll take the twenty dollars."

"Have you ever been up before me?"

"I don't know, judge. What time do you get up?"

"Aren't you ashamed to be seen here in this court so often?"

"Why, no, your Honor, I always thought it was a very respectable place."

"Why did you steal the eighty thousand dollars?"

"(Meekly) I was hungry."

*   *   *

"Prisoner at the bar, you've been convicted fourteen times of this offense. Aren't you ashamed to admit that?"

"Not particularly, your Honor. I don't think one ought to be ashamed of his convictions."

*   *   *

"All right," said the judge, "why did you steal that purse?"

"Your Honor, I was not feeling well, and I thought the change would do me good."

* * *

Michael Ueltzen, the sagacious Sacramento CPA, savors this side-splitter:

A Scotsman living on Long Island was charged with first degree murder. The jury came in with a verdict of guilty. At this point the defendant's attorney reached over to the unfortunate Scotsman and said, "Look, we can appeal to a higher court, but we'll need more money."

"But," said the defendant, "I don't want to spend any more money."

"Listen, it's either your money or your life!"

"It'll have to be my life," said the Scotsman. "I'm saving my money for my old age."

* * *

Judge: Have you anything to offer to the court before sentence is passed on you?

Prisoner: No, judge, I only had twelve dollars, but my lawyer took that.

* * *

I don't know what the crime rates are in other cities, but when it comes to armed robbery, New York wins—hands up!

—ALAN KING

* * *

Jury Jeers

A jury was being impaneled, and a prospective juror was questioned by the prosecutor.

"Do you know anything about this case?"

"No."

"Have you heard anything about it?"

"No."

"Have you read anything pertaining to this case?"

"No. I can't read."

"Have you formed any opinion about the case?"

"What case?"

"Accepted."

*   *   *

Headline from the *Oakland Tribune:*
TWO CONVICTS EVADE NOOSE.
JURY HUNG.

*   *   *

JURY

Twelve men or women or both who don't know their own minds, interfered with by a judge whose duty it is to let them decide for themselves.

* * *

In challenging a prospective juror, the prosecutor asked a milquetoast type, "Have you formed any opinion in this case?"

"No sir," he murmured, "I don't think my wife has read anything about the case yet."

* * *

Mrs. Lindhorst had been called for jury duty. She declined to serve because, she said, she did not believe in capital punishment. The judge tried to persuade her to stay. "Madam," he said, "this is not a murder case. It is merely a case in which a wife is suing her husband because she gave him ten thousand dollars to buy her a new fur coat, and he lost it all at the race track instead."

"I'll serve," agreed Mrs. Lindhorst. "I could be wrong about capital punishment."

* * *

Kirchner subpoenaed young Phelan as an important witness. First the lawyer asked, "Young man, have you an occupation?"

"Nope."

"Well then, what occupation does your father follow?"

"None," said Phelan.

"You tell us your father has no occupation. Does he ever do anything to support his family?"

"Well, he works once in a while," the boy replied.

"Then you mean your father is a lazy, worthless, good-for-nothing?"

"I don't know, sir," answered the witness, "You can ask him yourself. He's over there in the jury box."

*   *   *

O'Braddigan was on trial for stealing a gold shamrock and four shillelaghs. The case went to the jury on Monday, but as Friday drew to a close, the members of the jury were deadlocked: eleven for conviction and one for acquittal. The judge was impatient.

"Well, gentlemen," said the bailiff as he entered the jury room, "shall I order the usual twelve dinners?"

"No," snapped the foreman, "make it eleven dinners and one bale of hay!"

*   *   *

During the trial Judge Talbot asked a prospective juror if he had any opinion as to whether the prisoner was guilty or innocent. The man replied, "No, I have not, your Honor."

"And," continued the magistrate, "have you any conscientious scruples against capital punishment?"

The man said, "Ordinarily I have, but not in this case."

*   *   *

A judge, disgusted with the jury that seemed unable to reach a decision in a perfectly evident case, rose and said, "I discharge the jury."

The foreman of the jury bellowed, "You can't discharge me!"

The judge asked, "And why not?"

"Because," said the foreman, pointing at the defense lawyer, "I'm being hired by that man there!"

*   *   *

"You better come in quick.
They just voted eleven to one to
gang bang one of the jurors."

The Texas trial was over, and the jury returned from the deliberation. "Your Honor," said the foreman as he gave the verdict, "we find that the man who stole the mare is not guilty."

*　　*　　*

Rawley was called for jury duty and asked the judge to be dismissed because he was ill. The judge inquired what was wrong with him.

"I have the seven-year-itch, your Honor," he replied.

The judge turned to the clerk of court and said, "Scratch this man."

*　　*　　*

The prosecution and defense had both presented their final arguments in a case involving the maker of illegal Tennessee sour mash.

The judge turned to the jury and asked, "Before giving you your instructions, do any of you have any questions?"

"Yes, your Honor," replied one of the jurors. "Did the defendant boil the malt one or two hours, does he cool it quickly, and at what point does he add the yeast?"

*　　*　　*

"I couldn't serve as a juror, judge. One look at that fellow convinces me he's guilty."

"Sh-h! You're looking at the district attorney."

* * *

"Your Honor," said the foreman of the jury, "this good-lookin' lady is suing this man for ten thousand dollars for a stolen kiss."

"Correct," responded the judge. "You are to decide if it is worth it."

"That's the point, your Honor. How can we decide its value without a sample?"

* * *

Diet book author, Carol Robertson, tells about the two Scottsdale socialites having lunch at a chic cafe:

"Oh, Jennifer, can you imagine what's happened? I've got to serve on the Grand Jury."

"Me, too, Margaret."

"Of course, darling, you realize that our responsibilities will be heavy."

"Oh goodness yes. What shall we wear?"

* * *

All men are patriotic when they're called to serve on a jury in a bathing beauty contest.

*   *   *

Coleby, just out of college, was pleading his first case in South Carolina. A train had killed twenty-four pigs, and the young attorney was trying to impress the jury with the magnitude of the injury.

"Yes, gentlemen of the jury, twenty-four pigs. Imagine, twenty-four pigs. Twice the number there are in the jury box."

*   *   *

For two days, Judge Deborah Lippert had been hearing an important case involving two million dollars. On the third day, while the trial was in progress, she noticed that one of the jurors was missing.

"Mr. Foreman," she inquired, "where is the twelfth member of the jury? I see only eleven present."

"Your Honor," explained the foreman, "the missing man is Patrick O'Malley. He took the day off to march in the Saint Patrick's Day parade—but it's all right, he left his verdict with me!"

*   *   *

After serving a week on a jury, Caldwell was asked:

"You must've listened to so much law this past week, you're almost a lawyer yourself now."

"Yes," said the juryman, "I'm so full of law that I'm going to find it hard to keep from cheating people after I get back to business."

*　　*　　*

At a rape trial, Denise, the young victim, was asked by the D.A. what the defendant said before the alleged assault. Too embarrassed to answer aloud, Denise asked if she could write out the answer. After reading the note, the judge passed it along to the jurors.

One juror, who had dozed off, was nudged by the woman juror next to him. He took the note from her hand and read, "I'm going to fuck you like you've never been fucked before." The juror smiled to the woman and slipped the note in his pocket.

The judge said, "Will juror number twelve please pass the note back to me!"

"I can't, your Honor," he said. "It's too personal."

*　　*　　*

In Kansas, a jury convened to inquire into a case of murder. After sitting through the evidence, the twelve jurors retired and, after deliberating, returned with the following verdict:

"The jury is all of one mind—temporarily insane."

*   *   *

Some women take up the law and become lawyers. Other women lay down the law and become wives.

—JOAN RIVERS

Nuptial Nifties

Brian and Estelle had just finished a lovely dinner at a Boston restaurant.

Brian was trying to convince Estelle that marriage was the answer.

"It'll be very easy for us to get married," he said. "My father's a minister."

"Okay, let's give it a try," said the girl. "If it doesn't work out, mine's a lawyer."

*　　*　　*

Following is an excerpt of testimony given during a divorce proceeding:

"We were so happy for over a year, your Honor, and then baby came."

"Boy or girl?"

"Girl, your Honor. She was a blonde and moved in next door."

*   *   *

Judge: You say this woman shot her husband with his pistol and at close range?

Witness: Yessir, that's right.

Judge: Any powder marks on his body?

Witness: Yessir, that's why she shot him.

*   *   *

A Reno lawyer was confronted in his office by Mrs. Carmichael who said that she wanted a divorce.

"On what grounds?" asked the attorney.

She said she thought her husband was unfaithful to her.

"That's more like it," said the lawyer. "And what makes you think your husband isn't faithful?"

"Well," she said, "first of all, I don't think he's the father of my child."

*   *   *

A navy chief in Norfolk hauled Gilmer into police court with the charge that his wallet was lifted. "Yes, I'm guilty, judge," said Gilmer. "Please send me away, and while you're about it, give me a divorce, too."

"But why a divorce?" asked the magistrate.

The defendant answered, "I opened the chief's wallet, and the only things I found in it were three pictures of my wife."

* * *

Old man Grossman was with his Ft. Lauderdale attorney, drawing up his last will and testament. "I wanna leave all my worldly goods, property, and funds to my wife," instructed Grossman. "But only on the condition that she marries within a year."

"But Mr. Grossman," asked the lawyer, "why on that condition?"

"Because," answered the testator, "I want somebody to be sorry I died."

* * *

Mrs. Burber stood before the magistrate. "I was always having trouble with either my husband or the furnace, judge. Every time I'd watch one, the other would go out."

Jeanne Robertson, America's tallest funny lady, gets titanic titters with this tickler:

Mitchell, a small wisp of a man, was married to a domineering woman who was a head taller and outweighed him by a hundred pounds. One morning at breakfast in their Raleigh home, she began reading aloud from the newspaper.

"Here's a story of a Detroit woman who says that present marriage laws make woman the slave of man."

"Then why don't they enforce the law!" snapped Mitchell meekly.

Lawyer: In this will you really insist upon being buried at sea?

Client: Yes, I do. You see my wife says that when I'm dead she's going to dance on my grave.

*   *   *

During a divorce trial the husband's secretary was on the witness stand. The counsel for the defense asked her, "Are you married or unmarried?"

"Unmarried four times," replied the witness unblushingly.

*   *   *

The judge looked down at the woman and said, "What makes you think your husband is getting tired of you?"

"He hasn't been home for seven years," she said.

*   *   *

"Yes, Mrs. Fanelli, a divorce is possible," said the attorney, "but it will cost you about eight hundred dollars."

"That's too much money," said the woman. "Besides, I can have him shot for a quarter of the price."

*   *   *

François, a convict in the French penal colony serving a life sentence, wanted to marry one of the women convicts. Before permission was granted, the priest cross-examined the prisoner.

"Did you marry in France?"

"Yes, Father, I did, but my first wife is dead."

"Have you any evidence to show that she is dead?"

"No."

"Then," said the priest, "I cannot marry you. You must offer some proof that your wife is dead."

François said, "I can prove that my former wife is dead."

"And how can you do that?"

"I was sent here for killing her."

*   *   *

Wife: I want to know if I have grounds for a divorce.
Lawyer: Are you married?
Wife: Yes, of course.
Lawyer: Then you have grounds.

*   *   *

Hell hath no fury like the lawyer of a woman scorned.

*   *   *

Charlie Winkler, Nebraska's favorite humor dispenser, fractures folks with this tail wagger:

Wheeler was standing before a divorce judge swaying back and forth, obviously under the influence of alcohol.

The judge peered down at him and said, "Look at you . . . you're a bum. I'm going to give your wife a divorce, the house, your business, and the children, plus $350-a-month alimony."

"That's real nice of you, your Honor," sputtered Wheeler, "and to show you I'm not such a bad guy, I'm going to slip her a few bucks myself every now and then."

*   *   *

Brechman had just returned from a vacation in St. Tropez and was telling Doyle, his law partner, that the second day there, his wife fell off a horse and was knocked unconscious. "I called the doctor, and he examined her and said she would be unconscious for three weeks."

"What did you do?" asked Doyle.

"What could I do?" replied the lawyer. "I moved to a cheaper hotel."

*   *   *

ALIMONY

The screwing you get
for the screwing you got

* * *

Lieberman telephoned his client. "Josh, I've got good news and bad news. A jury has acquitted you and your wife has left you."

"So, what's the bad news?"

* * *

Stephanie went to court seeking a divorce.

"Do you have any grounds?" asked the judge.

"Yes," she replied. "I have half an acre."

The judge said, "Do you have a grudge?"

"No," answered the woman. "I have a carport."

"Does he beat you up?"

"No, I get up half an hour ahead of him every morning!"

"I don't know why you want a divorce," said the judge.

"We just can't communicate."

* * *

Lou Custrini, the corporate PR master-mind, gets guffaws with this goofy gleeful:

Aldridge and Dangler, members of two rival law firms, delighted in taking away one another's clients. Their rivalry often turned into personal abuse.

At a pretrial hearing, they found themselves seated side by side. Aldridge ran his hand over the other's bald head.

"You know, Dangler, your head feels exactly like my wife's ass!"

Dangler ran his hand over his own head and said, "You know, you're right."

Lawyer: Too bad about your client Buskin being sent up as an embezzler. Did he take his misfortune like a man?

Law Partner: You bet. He blamed his wife for everything.

* * *

"What are you cutting out of the paper?"

"It's a story about a Florida man securing a divorce because his wife went through his pockets."

"What are you going to do with it?"

"Put it in my pocket."

* * *

Mrs. Miller wanted a divorce. The judge asked, "What fault do you find with your husband?"

"Your Honor, he's a liar, a brute, a thief, and a brainless idiot."

"That's very serious," exclaimed his Honor. "Can you prove all that?"

"Prove it? Why, everybody knows it."

"If you knew all this, then why did you marry him?"

"I didn't know it before I married him."

The husband shouted, "She did too!"

* * *

They had fallen in love during a murder trial. But unfortunately the lawyer was married. The divorcée was heartsick.

"Oh, Brandon," she said, "isn't there some way we can go on seeing each other once the trial is finished?"

He exploded. "What's the matter with you? Do you want to go sneaking down back alleys and checking into tacky motel rooms? Is that what you want?"

"Of course not," she said.

"Oh," said the attorney. "Well, it was just a suggestion."

*   *   *

Magistrate: You know that it's against the law to speed?

Defendant: I do, your Honor.

Magistrate: Then as an old resident of this community, you ought to know that our laws are strictly enforced.

Defendant: You're right, your Honor. But this is what happened. Earlier in the afternoon, my wife phoned me that the women's church group would hold a rummage sale, so I was rushing home to save my last suit.

Magistrate: Case dismissed!

*   *   *

While away at an ABA convention, Geiger met Arlene, a pretty hostess who was chic and intelligent. When the attorney persuaded her to disrobe in his hotel room, he found out she had a superb body. Unfortunately, Geiger found himself unable to perform.

On his first night home, the lawyer padded naked from the shower into the bedroom to find his wife in a rumpled bathrobe, her hair curled, her face creamed, munching Godiva chocolates while she pored through *Ladies Home Journal.* And then he felt the onset of a magnificent erection.

Looking down at his throbbing member, he snarled, "You ungrateful, mixed-up son of a bitch. Now I know why they call you a prick!"

Miss Komorowski was named as the "other woman" in a divorce case. She sat on the witness stand as the lawyer began to question her.

"Miss Komorowski," he said, "do you admit you went to a motel with this man?"

"Yeah," said the Polish girl, "but I couldn't help it."

"Couldn't help it? Why not?"

"He deceived me."

"How did he do that?" asked the lawyer.

"Well," said the girl, "he told the clerk at the reception desk that I was his wife."

* * *

During his big divorce case Burnett had fallen in love with the woman in the suit. One night his wife awakened to hear him mumbling, "Darling, I love you. As soon as I can get a divorce, we'll get married."

Suddenly, Burnett awoke and, seeing his wife's angry face, turned over and continued, "I object, your Honor! That testimony is irrelevant!"

* * *

Ramsey applied for a divorce.

"On what grounds?" asked the judge.

"My wife is the cause, your Honor, she talks and talks and talks."

"That's not sufficient grounds for a divorce in this court."

"But your Honor, my wife, she talks and talks and talks and talks."

"Tell me, what does she talk about?"

Ramsey sighed. "She don't say."

*   *   *

Judge: You were called for jury duty?

Juror: Yes sir, I was.

Judge: Are you married or single?

Juror: Married five years last January, your Honor.

Judge: Now, have you formed or expressed any opinion?

Juror: Not for five years, I haven't.

*   *   *

A lawyer's wife was explaining how her husband truly loved her. "There I was last Sunday afternoon, painting the living room ceiling while Dan was watching a football game, and I fell off the ladder. And you know what? At halftime he called an ambulance."

*   *   *

Young Man: Your Honor, I would like to get married.

Judge: How old are you?

Young Man: I'm thirty, sir.

Judge: And where is the girl you want to marry, and how old is she?

Young Man: She's standing over there, and she's sixteen.

Judge: I'm sorry, I can't do a thing for you. The young lady is not of age.

Young Man: Would you mind telling that to the fellow standing over there by the door with that shotgun?

*　　*　　*

What's the best way to save a marriage? Go out and price a few divorce lawyers!

*　　*　　*

"Why do you want a divorce?" demanded Judge Sarah Whitcomb.

"My wife, your Honor, she insists on keeping her pet lamb in our bedroom, and the smell is so terrible I can't stand it any more."

"Why don't you open the windows then?"

"What, and let all my pigeons out?"

*　　*　　*

Mrs. Durkee, after hearing a long and eloquent plea by her lawyer in a divorce action, burst into tears at the conclusion of the summation.

"What's the trouble?" inquired her lawyer.

"Nothing," said the client. "I would never have known how much I suffered if I hadn't heard it this day."

*   *   *

"Tell me about your love life," said the psychiatrist.

"Well," said the lawyer's life, "my love life with my husband is just like the Fourth of July."

"You mean it's all firecrackers and skyrockets?"

"No, I mean it happens only once a year."

*   *   *

Brody was moaning to Elder, his law partner. "I'm very upset. My wife is into group sex."

Elder said, "I don't blame you for being angry."

"It's worse than that. They won't let me in the group."

*   *   *

Pappas, the city's most prominent attorney, was standing in front of the urinal in the man's locker room of his fashionable country club. Rodney, the black assistant golf pro, came up next to him. Pappas couldn't resisting taking a peek.

"It's true," admitted Pappas. "You black guys really are hung."

"It isn't only being black," replied Rodney. "We do exercises for it."

"What kind?" asked the lawyer.

"Well, for one thing, we slap our pricks five times every night before we get into bed."

Pappas decided to try it. His wife was already in bed when he got home. He undressed in the bathroom, crept in, then slapped his penis five times. He was crawling between the covers when his wife called out, "Rodney, is that you?"

The Lee Ho Wongs were a happy Chinese couple living in San Francisco until one day a blessed event came to the Wong house. The child had none of Lee's characteristics; in fact, the child didn't even have slanted eyes or straight black hair.

So, Lee Ho Wong sued for divorce and told the court that he believed a sailor was visiting his house while he was at work. The judge presiding over the trial finally said, "Divorce granted. Two Wongs don't make a White."

* * *

At the Dulles Airport departure gate, Kirinsky was bidding farewell to the man for whom he was handling a big case. Harrison, who was also boarding the plane to New York, overheard the lawyer saying, "You've been a wonderful host, Andy. Thanks for the use of your guest room.

"And thank your wife. She's great in bed. I really enjoyed making love to her."

"It's nothing. Have a good trip."

Once on the plane, Harrison approached the lawyer. "Excuse me," he said, "but I couldn't help overhearing. Did you really enjoy making love to his wife?"

"No," said the lawyer, "but I really need this case."

* * *

Mrs. Graham was sitting in a fashionable Beverly Hills shoe store trying on some new pumps. Suddenly, she noticed the salesman, who had been waiting on her, staring up her dress. "My God!" she exclaimed. "What are you doing?"

"That sure is pretty," said the wide-eyed shoe seller. "I'd like to get some ice cream, shove it up there, and eat!"

The woman threw a box of shoes at the man and stormed out of the shop. She hopped into her Mercedes 450 SL and rushed over to her husband's law office. Mrs. Graham ran past the receptionist, waved off his secretary, and barged into Mr. Graham's office.

"I have never been so insulted in my life," she exclaimed. "I want you to sue that store for every cent they've got."

"What happened?"

Mrs. Graham repeated what the clerk did and then shouted, "Never mind suing! I want you to go down there and beat the hell out of that bastard!"

"Well, honey," said the lawyer, "anybody who can eat that much ice cream, I'm not gonna pick on!"

*   *   *

He is a great lawyer—his client got the chair, but he got the voltage reduced.
                                   —MOREY AMSTERDAM

Nowadays a thoughtful girl saves a piece of her wedding cake for her divorce lawyer.

*   *   *

The wife of a leading Pittsburgh attorney was explaining why she wore a Medic-Alert band on her wrist. "It's been so long since Richard made love to me; if I were in an accident, he'd have trouble identifying the body."

*   *   *

Divorces are arranged so lawyers can live happily ever after.

*   *   *

Gallows Glee

Before hanging Alvarez, the warden asked the condemned man if he had any last words. "Let's get it over with," replied the prisoner.

The signal was given, and Alvarez was dropped through the platform. But he didn't die. They brought him back to the platform and dropped him again. Still he didn't die. He just bounced up and down. This went on and on. After the seventh time, the condemned man, eyeballs popping out of his head and covered with perspiration, gasped, "Let's get through with this. What am I, a a killer or a yo-yo?"

* * *

Zany Dick Patterson, Broadway's newest comedy star, gets roars with this rib-buster:

"Thirty years ago today my Uncle Romo was put to death in the electric chair."

"No kidding."

"This afternoon the whole family got together, went down to the cellar, and put a wreath around the fuse box."

*   *   *

Warden Lawler apologized to the prisoner. "I'm terribly sorry, but it seems we've kept you here a week too long."

"Ah—that's all right warden," said the convict. "Just take it off the next time."

*   *   *

Fitzgerald was sitting beside the deathbed of his lawyer, Dolan. The attorney knew he was doomed and said with a sigh, "Dear friend, I've a confession to make. A year ago I robbed you of $200,000 in your firm's merger deal, and I also put your firm's control in my possession. I talked your wife into divorcing you and—"

"It's all right, old friend," said Fitzgerald, "I poisoned you."

*   *   *

"It is the duty of the court to charge that the warden of the state penitentiary shall hold you in confinement until the twenty-eighth day of January next, when, between the hours of sunrise and sunset he shall put you to death by the electric chair. May the Lord have mercy on your soul."

"Can I ask a favor, your Honor?" said the prisoner.

"Yes," said Judge Castillo.

"I ain't got no quarrel with the date. I can get all prepared by then and make my peace with the Lord. But I can't see the point keepin' me settin' in that chair from sunrise plum 'til sunset."

* * *

Prosecutor: Now tell the court how you came to take the car.

Defendant: Well, it was parked in front of a cemetery, so I thought the owner was dead.

* * *

A visitor at Wisconsin State Prison asked a prisoner, "What's your name?"

The prisoner sneered, "4653."

"Is that your real name?"

"Naw," he said, "just my pen name."

* * *

Hassler was tried and convicted of first-degree murder. At San Quentin, the warden asked his prisoner, "Is there anything you'd like to eat before the execution?"

"Yeah, I'd like some mushrooms," said the condemned man. "I've always been afraid to try them in case I might be poisoned."

*   *   *

Benny and Spike, two Brooklyn burglars, were having a beer.

"Did youse git anything on da last job?" asked Benny.

"Naw, the character who lives in the joint is a lawyer," answered Spike.

"Gee, dat's tough luck," said Benny, "did youse lose anything?"

*   *   *

"My father knew he was going to die a month before his death."

"Who told him?"

"The judge!"

*   *   *

A Maryland judge received this card from a prison inmate, "Serving some wonderful time. Wish you were here."

*   *   *

One that robs shoe stores.

* * *

Bert Stitt, the retired insurance millionaire, tells about the high school arithmetic class where the teacher posed this problem:

"A wealthy man dies and leaves ten million dollars. One-fifth is to go to his wife, one-fifth to his son, one-sixth to his butler, and the rest to charity. Now, what does each get?"

"A lawyer," shouted a sharp coed.

* * *

Chaplain: My man, I will allow you five minutes of grace before they hang you.

Condemned Man: That's not very long, but bring her in.

* * *

Did you hear about the sharp Philadelphia lawyer who got his client a suspended sentence?

They hanged him!

* * *

Bowdin arrived at the Franklin Penitentiary.

"How many years you get?" asked a fellow prisoner.

"Fifteen," said Bowdin.

"What'd you do?"

"Nothin'. Really nothin'."

"Come off it," said the other prisoner. "Nowadays you only get five for really nothin'."

*　　*　　*

A funeral director noticed an old man walking away from a funeral service. "A friend of yours?"

"Yes, he was my law partner."

"That's unfortunate," said the director. "Tell me, sir, how old are you?"

The elderly barrister said, "Ninety-two-years old."

"Well," said the mortician, "hardly worth going home, is it?"

*　　*　　*

"It all went on wine, women, and lawyers!"

Give a convict enough rope and he'll skip.

*　　*　　*

Mrs. Dawson, the dowager, while visiting the state prison, asked a convict, "Poor man, why are you here?"

"Because, lady," said the con, "my lawyer inherited eighty thousand dollars the day before he made his plea to the jury and he couldn't cry."

*　　*　　*

The jailbird was explaining why he was in prison. "It was a case of mistaken identity," he said. "I didn't know he was a cop."

*　　*　　*

A Boston police strike caused problems. A wanted criminal planned to give himself up—but he refused to cross a picket line.

*　　*　　*

A rich uncle died and left a will. One line read as follows: "I leave to my beloved nephew all the money he owes me."

*　　*　　*

Machlin, the town's only attorney, was summoned to the bedside of a dying man who wanted to make out his will.

"To my son, Lloyd, I leave forty thousand dollars. To my daughter, Janet, I bequeath twenty thousand dollars—"

"Wait a minute," interrupted the lawyer. "Your estate isn't worth more than eight thousand dollars. How do you suppose the beneficiaries are going to get the money?"

"Get it?" he shouted. "Let 'em work for it, same as I had to do!"

* * *

Where there's a will, there's a relative.

* * *

The lawyer was reading the will of the departed millionaire to the relatives who had gathered in his office. "And to my nephew, who asked that he be remembered," the lawyer read, "I want to say, 'Hello, Harold.' "

* * *

Did you hear about the Ozark hillbilly who passed away and left his estate in trust for his grieving wife?

She can't touch it 'till she's thirteen.

* * *

131

"My dear, I want you to know that I've just conferred with my lawyer, and I've put you down in my will for $100,000."

"Oh Auntie, darling, what can I say to thank you? Incidentally, how are you feeling today?"

* * *

Judith Briles, the brilliant young financial advisor, bubbles over this beauty:

"I want you to understand," said young Kostopoulous, "that I got my money by hard work. It took a long time; and when I say hard work, I mean hard work."

"Hey, I thought it was left to you by your rich uncle!"

"That's true, but I had to work to get it away from the lawyers. And brother, that was hard."

* * *

Steven and Boyd met on San Francisco's Castro Street. "Darling," exclaimed Steven, "I thought they'd sent you to jail on that sodomy charge?"

"Oh, no," said Boyd, "I found this wonderful lawyer who got the charge reduced to 'following too closely.'"

* * *

Monsieur Foucard, a leading solicitor from Paris, was visiting friends in St. Louis. At a dinner party, a Missouri lawyer smiled at him and teased, "All French law cases are always about sex!"

"That's not true, monsieur," said the Frenchman. "Take the case I'm handling now. It's simply a family problem. My client, Claude Philippe, was in love with Josette, but she was afraid of losing her virginity and made him promise he wouldn't penetrate her maidenhead.

"Claude Philippe did exactly as he promised, but just at that special moment, Josette's mother burst into the bedroom, saw what was going on, became furiously angry, and gave Claude Philippe a tremendous kick in the behind.

"He relieved himself, the girl got pregnant, and my client claims that the girl's mother is the father of the child!"

*   *   *

A lawyer attended the funeral of the richest man in town. A friend, arriving late, took a seat beside him and whispered, "How far has the service gone?"

The lawyer pointed to the minister in the pulpit and replied, "He just opened for the defense."

*   *   *

Gillmer took Kristine, the pretty young receptionist his firm just hired, to a motel room. The girl seemed shy and inexperienced, so the man decided he would be her tutor in the art of love. Gillmer began running his hands over her chest. "Do you know what I'm doing?" he asked.

"No," replied Kristine.

"I'm fondling your breasts."

Then he moved his hand down between her legs and asked, "Do you know what I'm doing now?"

When she replied, "No," he explained he was caressing her clitoris. Then he became so aroused that he spread her legs and thrust himself into her.

"Do you know what I'm doing now?" he panted.

"Yes," said Kristine, "you're catching herpes."

*　　*　　*

Conklin was leaving the cemetery after visiting his mother's grave. Suddenly, he stopped before a huge tombstone that read:

HERE LIES A LAWYER,
AND AN HONEST MAN

"How do you like that?" he murmured, "times are so bad, they're putting them two in a grave."

134

*　　*　　*

When old man Flintock's lawyer learned that his client had inherited a million dollars, he remarked to his secretary, "I'll have to break it gently or the old codger will drop dead from the shock."

At four o'clock the aged man was wheeled into the lawyer's office. "Mr. Flintock," began the barrister, "what would you say if I told you that you had inherited a million dollars?"

"What would I say?" repeated the old man. "Why, you damn fool, I'd say, 'half of it goes to you.'"

The lawyer dropped dead.

*　　*　　*

What's the difference between a dead lawyer and a dead snake lying in the road?

There are skid marks leading up to the snake.

*　　*　　*

A suburban widow was discussing her troubles with her best friend. "Don't talk to me about lawyers," said she. "I've had so much trouble over John's property that sometimes I wish he hadn't died."

*　　*　　*

Louie, the lip was going to die in the electric chair. He telephoned his lawyer for some last minute advice.

"What should I do?" asked the convict.

"Don't sit down!" said the attorney.

A lawyer will sometimes stay up all night just to break a widow's will.

* * *

Jackie Gayle, the popular nightclub funny man, gets screams with this line at a late night Vegas show:

"I've got a great lawyer. He got Ray Charles a driver's license."

* * *

Where there's a will, prosperity is just around the corner.

* * *

Steve Wozniak, the comedic computer whiz, gets howls with this hunk of hyperbole:

An attorney named Strange was asked what he would like to have inscribed on his tombstone.

"Just put 'Here lies an honest lawyer,' " he said.

"But," said the friend, "that really doesn't tell who it is."

"Sure it does," said the attorney, "Passersby will read it and say, 'That's Strange.' "

Bar Baubles

For three years Barrow, a young attorney, had been vacationing at a remote Vermont country inn. The last time, he'd finally managed an affair with the innkeeper's daughter. Now he arrived once again looking forward to an exciting few days. As he stopped his BMW in front of the inn, his heart almost stopped. There sat the girl with an infant on her lap!

"Rita, why didn't you write that you were pregnant?" he cried. "We could have gotten married, and the baby would have my name!"

"Well," she said, "when my folks found out about my condition, we sat up all night talkin' and talkin' and decided it'd be better to have a bastard in the family than a lawyer."

Santa Claus, the tooth fairy, an honest lawyer, and an old drunk are walking down the street together when they simultaneously spot a hundred dollar bill. Who gets it? The old drunk, of course; the other three are mythological creatures.

*   *   *

Chabot and Brock were having lunch at the Beverly Hills Hotel.

"As soon as I realized it was a crooked deal, I got out of it," said Chabot.

"How much?"

*   *   *

The ultimate in legal bills was received by a Hollywood restaurant owner. His attorney sent him a bill for eighty dollars "for waking up in the middle of the night and thinking about your case."

*   *   *

A lawyer was trying to persuade his friend to undergo analysis. "It's helped me tremendously," he said. "I was arrogant, vain, overbearing—"

His friend looked up. "That was *before* analysis?"

*   *   *

A cruise ship was wrecked in a storm. Next morning, the survivors found themselves on a deserted island without food or water. They noticed the wreckage of the ship on a sandbar only two hundred yards from the shore, but there were sharks swimming all around the inlet.

"I'll swim out and get food," volunteered a young man. "I used to be a lifeguard."

He dove into the water and in a few minutes was attacked and devoured by the sharks. Another man stepped forward. "I'm only a CPA, but I'm a strong swimmer. I can make it."

But he didn't. Thirty yards offshore, the sharks tore him apart. Suddenly, up stepped a paunchy, bespectacled, bald-headed man. "I'm an attorney, and I think I can get to the ship."

He entered the water and immediately eight sharks formed a two-lane escort and helped him to the ship, then back to the beach unharmed.

"It's a miracle!" shouted one of the passengers.

"Miracle, hell!" said the lawyer. "It's just professional courtesy."

* * *

A lawyer in a Reno motel answered the cries for help of a pretty airline hostess. He found her tied to the bedpost in her room, her clothes in shreds. She blurted out her sorry tale.

"Three men broke into my room, they tied me to the bedpost and then each one ravaged me."

The lawyer locked the door and dropped his pants.

"I'm sorry, honey," he said, "this just isn't your day."

Logan was questioning his client:

"Did you present your bill to the defendant, Mr. Kalkin?"

"Yes, sir."

"And when you did this, what did he say?"

"He told me to go to the devil."

"And what did you do then?"

"Why, I came right to you."

*　　*　　*

Metzger was invited to lecture at a law class at Harvard Law School. After completing the lecture, the attorney concluded by saying, "May God help you become truly learned in the law."

The students shouted, "The same to you."

*　　*　　*

Lawyer: Are you sure you can prove to the satisfaction of the court that my client is insane?

Doctor: Why certainly. And what is more, if you are ever in trouble and need my services, I'll do the same thing for you, too.

*　　*　　*

Returning to his seat at the L.A. Forum, popcorn in hand, an obese Brentwood divorce attorney leaned over and asked a woman, "Did I step on your feet when I came out?"

"Well," said the woman, prepared for an apology, "as a matter of fact you did."

"Good," he said, "then this is my row."

*   *   *

Dr. Jim Seidel, the Los Angeles pediatric specialist, loves this lollapalooza:

Gilbert and Freeman were discussing conditions in the legal profession. "How's business?" asked Gilbert.

"Absolutely rotten!"

"What now?"

"It's most discouraging," Freeman replied. "I just chased an ambulance twelve miles and found a lawyer in it."

*   *   *

How can you tell when a lawyer is lying?

His lips are moving.

*   *   *

An overbearing, pompous lawyer was unfolding his life's story to Nichols, a fellow attorney. "Yes, I've had a trying but rewarding life. When I was a child my mother said I would be a lawyer."

"Really?"

"Yes, and my misguided father said I would be a bum!"

Nichols said, "So you made them both happy and you became a bum lawyer."

* * *

The young lawyer was putting a diamond ring on his girlfriend's finger. "I'd like you to have this. It was my mother's."

"Gosh," she said, "your mother's engagement ring!"

"Yeah," he said, "She put up a hell of a fight, but I finally got it off her finger."

* * *

Lawyer: (Handing check for one hundred dollars to client who had been awarded five thousand dollars.) There's the balance after deducting my fee. What are you thinking of? Aren't you satisfied?

Client: I was just wondering who got hit by the car, you or me?

"How are you getting along with the law business?"

"I have one client."

"Is he rich?"

"He was."

*   *   *

Nick Carter, the congenial Nightingale Conant Communications V.P., connects with this winner:

Sean was brought to court and charged with burglary, and his wife, Maggie, was being cross-examined by Pratly.

"Did you know that this man was a burglar when you married him?" asked the lawyer.

"I did," replied Maggie.

"Then why on earth did you marry him?" persisted Pratley.

"Well," said Maggie, "I was gettin' on a bit and didn't want to be left on the shelf. I had the choice between a burglar and a lawyer, so I married the burglar."

"No further questions," said the attorney.

*   *   *

Dr. Hoffman, a psychiatrist, began testing dogs to see if they picked up any characteristics from their owners. So he got an architect's dog, an accountant's dog, and a lawyer's dog.

First the shrink put the architect's dog in a room with a big pile of dog biscuits. Through a one-way window, Hoffman observed what went on. The architect's dog built a little skyscraper out of biscuits, then a couple of tiny houses, and a small bridge.

Next he put the CPA's dog in the room with the biscuits. The dog divided the pile into two equal halves. The dog then took two biscuits from one pile and added them to the next pile, then took two biscuits from that pile and added them to the next one.

Then the doctor was ready for the next dog. But the lawyer's dog was a half hour late. He finally arrived, ate all the biscuits, screwed the other two dogs, then took the rest of the day off.

148

When asked, "What is a contingent fee?" the lawyer replied, "A contingent fee means that if I don't win your suit, I get nothing. If I do win it, you get nothing."

*   *   *

Did you hear about the sexy female attorney who consistently breaks speed limits but never gets a ticket?

Every time a policeman stops her, she simply lays down the law.

*   *   *

What do you need when you have three lawyers up to their necks in cement?

More cement.

*   *   *

The defense counsel had just finished his closing summation to the jury and was very much pleased with his presentation. Returning to his associates, he proudly said, "How did you like that? The jury is in tears."

"Yes," replied an associate, "they realize that your poor client hasn't a chance in the world."

*   *   *

A young lawyer spent most of his time trying to appear busy and prosperous. He went out for a while, leaving on his door a card neatly marked: "Will be back in an hour." On his return he found that some mischievous rival had inscribed on the sign, "What for?"

*   *   *

Fred Feuille, the masterful marketing director, doubles up pals with this doozy:

The gate between heaven and hell broke, and St. Peter called to the devil, "It's your turn to fix it."

"Sorry," said the devil. "We're too busy fixing our heating system to worry about a little thing like a gate."

"If you don't fix it," said St. Peter, "I'll have to sue you for breaking our working agreement."

"Is that so!" said the devil. "Where are you going to find a lawyer?"

*   *   *

Young Attorney: And if it please the court, if I am wrong in this, I have another point that is equally conclusive.

*   *   *

A cannibal walked into a neighborhood butcher store and was trying to make up his mind on what to buy for dinner. He saw a sign that read: "Accountants' Brains, $4.95 a pound." Then another that said: "Lawyers' Brains, $50 a pound."

"Say, mister," asked the cannibal, "'why are lawyers' brains so expensive?"

"Well," said the cannibal butcher, "do you know how many attorneys we have to kill to get a pound of brains?"

"Pardon me," said the visitor, "are you a resident here?"

"Yes," was the answer. "I've lived here going on some fifty years. What can I do for you?"

"I'm in some trouble with the law and I'm looking for a criminal lawyer. Have you any here?"

"Well," said the old timer, "we're pretty sure we have, but we can't prove it."

*　　*　　*

Kessler called on another attorney and asked his opinion on a certain point of law. Whereupon the lawyer said, "I generally get paid for what I know."

Kessler took a half-dollar from his pocket and offered it. "Tell me all you know and give me the change."

*　　*　　*

Young Siebold asked an old lawyer how he could attain success as a criminal lawyer. "Young fellow," advised the old practitioner, "always collect your fee in advance; and always remember that you will not be required to serve the sentence."

*　　*　　*

Roberta rushed into the house and told her mom that since her boyfriend had just passed his bar exams, they wanted to get married.

"Don't you think it'd be a good idea for him to practice for a year first?" asked the woman.

"But, mother," she replied, "we have been practicing!"

*   *   *

Hamner, the advertising exec, began shouting at his pretty secretary.

"We may have been to bed a few times together, but who said you could be late for work?"

"My lawyer," said the girl.

*   *   *

Comedian Robert Klein, in his critically acclaimed one-man show, makes this poignant comment:

We set an amoral table in the serving of justice: Smoke a joint in Texas, and you get sent away for two years. Commit a murder in Rhode Island, and you can't watch television for three nights.

*   *   *

The pope and a lawyer died at the same time and were standing at the gates of heaven. St. Peter said, "We've been expecting you. Your rooms are ready." Then he said to the lawyer, "Excuse me while I take the pope to his room. I will return presently and then show you to your quarters."

"Would you mind if I tag along?" asked the lawyer.

"Not at all," said St. Peter.

They arrived at the pope's room. It had a twin bed, a single chair, a little table, a small radio and looked very much like a room in a Holiday Inn.

St. Peter then took the lawyer to his room. He was shocked to see a palatial suite with balcony, king-sized bed, spiral staircase, color TV console with remote control, stereo, VCR, plush carpeting, Jacuzzi, and a sauna.

"This room is terrific!" exclaimed the attorney. "But why is it that the pope, the leader of the entire Roman Catholic Church, got only a standard room, and I got this wonderful penthouse?"

"Well," said St. Peter, "we've had many popes up here, but you're the first lawyer to ever make it!"

*   *   *

Elsworth arrived before the Pearly Gates and was startled by his reception. As he strolled up to the gate, he was greeted by a fifty-piece orchestra. Two hundred little girls tossed rose petals in his path, and he was welcomed by St. Peter with open arms.

"I'm really surprised at this greeting," offered the lawyer.

"Well," replied St. Peter. "You're a very special person."

"I don't understand," said the attorney.

"Oh," explained St. Peter, "you're the oldest lawyer who has ever entered our Gates. "You're 174 years old."

"I think you're a little mixed up there, St. Peter. I'm only 46."

"But, you see, we don't go by chronological age. We count your years by the number of hours you've billed your clients."

*　　*　　*

Ignorance of the law does not prevent the losing lawyer from collecting the bill.

*　　*　　*

LAW FIRM

Dewey, Cheatham, and Howe

*　　*　　*

Did you hear about the lady lawyer who moonlighted as a callgirl? She was a prostituting attorney.

* * *

What is it a swan can do easily, a duck can do with little effort, and an attorney should definitely do?
Stick his bill up his ass.

* * *

At the graduation exercises, Paul accepted his law degree and approached his parents to receive their congratulations. Paul placed his hand on his father's shoulder, and the new lawyer said, "Pop, it's time for a change. All your life you worked hard for me, now it's time for you to go out and work hard for yourself."

Litigator Levity

Two Atlanta attorneys were discussing a prospective client. They were undecided as to whether to accept the account.

"Before we do anything, tell me, has he any money?"

His partner said, "He's worth in the neighborhood of a million dollars."

"Good. We take the case."

"Really?"

"Yes, that's my favorite neighborhood," said the attorney.

* * *

Lawyer: I've just landed that big corporation law case for my son.

Partner: But the boy is only three years old.

Lawyer: Certainly, but he'll be ready for it by the time I've finished the preliminary work of getting a jury.

* * *

PROBATE

A place where lawyers recline
while they are waiting to get the money.

* * *

Boggs was in need of legal advice. Before he presented his case, he asked Linzy what the fee structure would be.

"Well," said the lawyer, "I charge twenty dollars for advising you to do just what the law permits you to do. For offering advice about how you can safely do what the law forbids, my minimum fee is two hundred dollars."

* * *

Reverend Curtis has engaged the services of Jacqueline Mahler and soon received a bill. The clergyman went to see the lawyer.

"I always understood that you gentlemen of the bar were not in the habit of charging men of the cloth for your services."

"Allow me to correct you," replied Miss Mahler. "You look for your reward in the next world, but we lawyers have to get ours in this."

* * *

"Your office is as hot as an oven," said the prospective client to his lawyer.

"So it should be. After all, this is where I make my bread."

*   *   *

Cy Eberhart, the smiling Salem clergyman, cracks up the congregation with this cutie:

Reverend Kilgore and Werner, an attorney, sat next to each other on a jet to Phoenix.

"Do you ever make mistakes in pleading?" asked the minister.

"I do," replied Werner.

"And what do you do about them?" inquired Reverend Kilgore.

"Why, if large ones, I mend them; if small ones, I let them go," said the lawyer. "Do you ever make mistakes in preaching?"

"Yes, I have."

"And what do you do?" asked Werner.

"I dispose of them in the same manner as you do," answered the holy man. "Recently, as I was preaching, I meant to say that the devil was 'the father of liars,' but instead I said, 'the father of lawyers.' The mistake was so small that I let it go."

*   *   *

Client: I know the evidence is strongly against me, but I have $75,000 to fight the case. Can we win?

Lawyer: As your attorney, I assure you that you'll never go to prison with that amount of money.

Dottie Walters, America's uncrowned queen of the speaking profession, woos audiences with this whimsical whopper:

Attorney Alice Garber was called to try a lawsuit in a small Alabama town. There was not much doing, and after finishing her business, the lawyer got very lonesome. As she paid her hotel bill, she said to the manager, "I intend, if possible, to come to this town to end my days."

"Really," said the manager, "Ahm glad that yawl like our town so well."

"You misunderstand," said Miss Garber. "The reason I want to end my days here is because it seems to me that after a woman had lived here awhile, death would be a welcome relief."

*   *   *

The county's brightest attorney left the banquet hall with a look of self satisfaction. One of his colleagues stopped him and said, "Congratulations, Maury."

"Thank you! Thank you very much."

"Were you surprised when you got the nomination as president of the Bar Association?"

"I'll say. My acceptance speech nearly fell out of my hand."

*   *   *

First Lawyer: Possession is nine-tenths of the law.

Second Lawyer: Tried any drug cases lately?

*   *   *

Sambito was in jail for murder, rape, blackmail, and kidnapping. When the court-appointed lawyer went to see him, he had a gleam in his eye.

"I think I found a loophole. In the case of Farrell versus Lemongella, April 12, 1912, Volume V, page 246, paragraph 6, I think I got the answer. Don't worry about a thing, I'll get you out of this murder-rape-blackmail-kidnapping mess. Just leave it to me."

"Great," said the prisoner.

"Now, I'm leaving for Miami Monday," said the lawyer, "and I'll be back Friday. Meanwhile, try to escape."

*   *   *

Twitchell, when pleading the cause of an infant, took the child in his arms and presented it to the jury with a torrent of tears flowing from the boy's eyes. This had a great effect. But the opposing counsel asked the child what made him cry.

"He pinched me," said the youngster.

*   *   *

"Who is the best lawyer in town?"

"Frank Reardon, when he is sober."

"And who is the second best lawyer in town?"

"Frank Reardon, when he is drunk."

* * *

Flaherty, a brilliant Boston lawyer, was noted for his capacity to put away large quantities of John Barleycorn. One day he stumbled into the courtroom cockeyed.

"Mornin' yer Honor. Hozza boy?" he bellowed.

The judge stared at him for a moment and then thundered, "Get out of here. You're drunk, sir!"

The attorney picked up his briefcase, and replied, "Thass right, yer Honor, and thass the firs' correct decision I've heard in thish court."

* * *

O'Connor became a lawyer and was defending his first client in a murder trial. As he was making his final speech for the defense, he sent a note to a friend, an eminent lawyer present in the courtroom. "What are the chances of my client being acquitted?"

"Keep talking," answered the friend. "The longer you talk, the longer your client has to live."

LAWSUIT

A matter of expense and suspense.

*   *   *

No book of laughs about the legal profession would be complete without some words on the subject from the wonderfully wacky comic Steven Wright:

I was caught for a parking ticket. I pleaded insanity. I said, "Your honor, why would anyone in their right mind park in the passing lane?"

I broke a mirror in my house. You're supposed to get seven years bad luck, but my lawyer thinks he can get me five.

*   *   *

Axelrod was advising his pretty actress client. "When we go to court, I want you to wear a short skirt."
"But they're not in style," she protested.
"Do you want to be acquitted?" asked the lawyer. "Or do you want to be in style?"

*   *   *

The case was coming to a close, and attorney Stoddard approached the jury box to sum up.

"Gentlemen of the jury, the plaintiff called my client, Mr. Swenson, a two-faced Swedish conniving bastard. Now, Mr. Rizzutti, if he had called you a two-faced Italian conniving bastard, what would you have done? And you, Mr. Berkowitz, if he called you a two-faced conniving Jewish bastard? Or any of you, gentlemen, what would you have done if he had called you the kind of two-faced conniving bastards you all are?"

Mahaffey visited a seriously ill lawyer in the hospital. He found him sitting up in bed, frantically leafing through the Bible.

"What are you doing?" asked Mahaffey.

"Looking for loopholes," replied the lawyer.

*   *   *

Bill Gove, the mirthful sales motivator, mines merriment with this winner:

In Japan there's one lawyer for every 15,000 people—opposed to the United States where there's one lawyer to every 1,500. I've got a way to solve the balance of payments problem. They ship us a Toyota, and we ship them a lawyer.

*   *   *

"I can beat this case," Stenhouse told his client.

"What do I do?" asked the client.

"Just do what I tell you," said the lawyer, "plead insanity."

"Insanity?"

"Yeah—you got a much better chance of busting out of the nut house than the can."

*   *   *

Judge Tsing called for a short recess. His Honor then advised the attorney, "Why not withdraw with your client to give him the benefit of your best advice."

When the trial resumed, the attorney returned to the courtroom without his client.

"Where's the prisoner?" demanded the judge.

"He's gone," answered the lawyer. "That was the best advice I could give him."

* * *

Bill Petersen, one of Chicago's most brilliant legal minds, beams over this bauble:

Attorney Martha McGraw, who was quite short, appeared in court as a witness. She was cross-examined by lawyer Bryant, who was over six feet five inches tall. Bryant asked the witness, "What is your profession?"

"I'm a member of the bar."

"You're a lawyer," said the giant counselor, "why I could put you in my vest pocket."

"You probably could," snapped Miss McGraw, "but if you did, you'd have more law in your vest pocket than you ever had in your head."

* * *

Young Jeff was in court on his first offense. The complaint charged that he stole ten bicycles. Feinstein, his lawyer, made this suggestion to the court. "Your Honor, this is the boy's first offense. If he paid for the stolen articles, would it be all right with the court?"

After considerable discussion by the plaintiff and the judge, it was agreed that the case would be dropped.

Then Feinstein jumped up and asked, "Should the boy pay for the ten bicycles at wholesale or retail prices?"

*   *   *

Walking out of a Kansas City court, Bedrosian said to his associate, "I feel like telling that judge where to get off again."

"What do you mean, again?"

"I felt like it last week."

*   *   *

"What was the most confusing case you ever had?" asked the physician of the barrister.

"Case of champagne," returned the lawyer. "I hadn't got half through it before I was all muddled up."

*   *   *

Moffit was being tried on charges of indecent assault, rape, and driving without lights. His lawyer claimed that the rape charge was absurd. "Good heavens," he said, "the girl stopped my client's car on the highway with her leg, which she used to thumb a lift. And when my client drove on, the girl deliberately jumped into the back seat with him."

* * *

Mary Jo Crowley, the cute California comic, contends lawyers are replacing laboratory rats in popularity among scientific researchers. "There are more of them," says Crowley, "and you don't get so emotionally attached."

* * *

Judge: (Leaving the courtroom) I've lost my hat.
Lawyer: That's nothing. I lost a suit here yesterday.

* * *

He was one of the best lawyers money could buy. He not only knew the law—he knew the judge, too.

* * *

Russell Nelson, the popular Arizona State University Prexy, prompts pleasure with this piece of persiflage:

The church was jammed for the eleven A. M. Sunday service. Preacher Sanderson delivered his sermon with great conviction and concluded with the question, "In time of trial, what brings us the greatest comfort?"

An eager young attorney rose to his feet and shouted, "An acquittal!"

A merchant retained an attorney to defend him in a suit for damages brought by an employee. Unfortunately for the attorney, his client lost the suit by furnishing evidence on the stand that was favorable to the prosecution to the tune of about ten thousand dollars.

The merchant, naturally indignant, said, "If I had a son born an idiot, I'd make him a lawyer."

"Your father seems to have been of another opinion," rejoined the lawyer.

*   *   *

Heather Florence, publishing's most popular legal practitioner, prefers this pleasantry:

Tiffany Silverstein walked into a Madison Avenue shoe store in New York one afternoon and said, "Give me a pair of pumps two sizes too small for me."

"Two sizes too small?" asked the sales clerk. "What's the idea?"

"I've got trouble. Nothing but trouble," said the lawyer. "I just lost my third case in court, my partner is leaving me to join another firm, and I've been threatened with disbarment. So, the only pleasure I have left is to go home at night and take off my tight shoes."

O'Branahan, addicted to imbibing freely and often, was arrested for selling home-stilled whiskey. His lawyer put him on the stand and asked the jurors to look carefully at the Irishman.

"Now, ladies and gentlemen of the jury," concluded the lawyer, "you've looked carefully at the defendant. Can you sit there in the jury and honestly believe that if my client had a quart of whiskey he would sell it?"

He was acquitted.

* * *

Lawyer Gail Pruitt had a disagreement with the presiding judge and turned her back to the bench and returned to her table.

"Are you trying to show your contempt for this court, counsel?" demanded the judge.

"No, your Honor," said the attorney, "I'm trying to conceal it."

* * *

I learned law so well, the day I graduated I sued the college, won the case, and got my tuition back.

—FRED ALLEN

* * *

Lawyers have a particular way of expressing themselves. They'll never come right out and say, "My client is guilty. He told me so." They have a way of twisting things around to the jury:

"My client is alleged to have killed his wife. He is supposed to have chopped up her body into little pieces, and stuffed them into a suitcase. He was apprehended trying to cross the border into Mexico when someone noticed that a piece of her thumb was sticking out of the suitcase.

"Now ladies and gentlemen of the jury, I know what you're thinking. You're thinking my client is a beast, a killer, a maniac. Well, I don't see him that way. A sloppy packer, maybe . . ."

*　　*　　*

Barney and Zack were walking down Broadway when they spotted Carol, an attractive hooker. Barney said to his friend, "I'd give a hundred bucks to spend the night with her."

Carol turned and said, "I'll take you up on that."

Barney left his pal and went straight to Carol's apartment. Next morning Barney gave the call girl fifty dollars and started to leave. She demanded the rest of the money. "If you don't give me the other fifty, I'll sue you!''

. Barney laughed, ''That I'd like to see.''

Three days later he was served a summons to appear in court. Barney hurried to his lawyer, McNally, and told him what happened. McNally said, ''She can't get a judgment against you on such grounds, but it'll be interesting to see how her case'll be presented.''

After the usual preliminaries, Carol's lawyer, Marlow, addressed the court: ''Your Honor, my client is the owner of a piece of property, a garden spot surrounded by a profuse growth of shrubbery, which property she agreed to rent to the defendant for a specified length of time for the sum of one hundred dollars. The defendant took possession of the property, used it extensively for the purpose for which it was rented, but upon evacuating the premises, he paid only fifty dollars. The rent is not excessive since it was restricted property, and we ask judgment to assure payment of the balance.''

Barney's lawyer said, ''Your Honor, my client agrees the young lady has a fine piece of property, for a degree of pleasure was derived from the transaction. However, my client found a well on the property around which he placed his own stones, sunk a shaft, and erected a pump, all labor being personally performed by him. We claim these improvements to the property are sufficient to offset the unpaid balance, and that the plaintiff was adequately compensated for the rental of the said property. We therefore ask judgment not be granted.''

Carol's lawyer said, "Your Honor, my client agrees that the defendant did find a well on the property, and he did make improvements such as described by my opponent; however, had the defendant not known the well existed, he would never have rented the property; also, on evacuating the premises, the defendant moved the stones, pulled out the shaft, and took the pump with him. In so doing, he not only dragged his equipment through the shrubbery, but left the hole much larger than it was prior to his occupancy, making it easily accessible to little children. We therefore ask judgment be granted.''

She got it.

About the Author

This is the 38th "Official" joke book by Larry Wilde. With sales of more than nine million copies, it is the largest selling humor series in publishing history.

Larry Wilde has been making people laugh for over thirty years. As a stand-up comedian, he has performed in top night spots with stars such as Debbie Reynolds, Pat Boone and Ann-Margaret.

His numerous television appearances include "The Tonight Show," "The Today Show," "Merv Griffin," and "The Mary Tyler Moore Show."

Larry's two books on comedy technique, *The Great Comedians Talk About Comedy* (Citadel) and *How the Great Comedy Writers Create Laughter* (Nelson-Hall), are acknowledged as the definitive works on the subject and are used as college textbooks.

A recognized authority on comedy, Larry is also a motivational speaker. In his humorous keynote speeches for corporations, associations, and medical facilities, he advocates getting more out of life by developing a better sense of humor.

Larry Wilde is the founder of National Humor Month, celebrated across the U.S. to emphasize the valuable contribution laughter makes to the quality of our lives. It begins each year on April Fools' Day.

He lives on the northern California coast with his wife Maryruth.